THE DESCENT OF ISHTAR

both the Sumerian and Akkadian versions

*also includes 'The Epic of Anzu'
and 'Erra and Ishum'*

TIMOTHY J. STEPHANY

ISBN-13: 978-1517611361
ISBN-10: 1517611369

Printed in the United States of America by Createspace

http://www.timothyjstephany.com

Contents

other books by TIMOTHY J. STEPHANY

The Gilgamesh Cycle

Enuma Elish: The Babylonian Creation Epic

The Holy Bible Revealed I: Genesis through Kings with Sources

The Holy Bible Revealed II: Compositional History

The Yahweh Document: The Holy Bible's First Edition

The Levi Document: The Earliest Biblical Source

The Eden Enigma: A Dialogue

Roar of the Tempests: A Dialogue

The Death of King David: A Dialogue

The Zodiac Mysteries

Blood & Incest: The Unholy Beginning of the Universe

Introduction

The Mesopotamian Queen of Heaven, known as Ishtar among the Akkadians and Inanna among the Sumerians, is broadly associated with the heavenly sphere, but specifically identified with the Morning Star and Evening Star, as her hymns declare:

> At dusk hour the bright star, that mighty light pervading heaven,
> The Evening Lady makes her appearance in the sky's firmament[1]

> My Lady gazes down in satisfaction from the sky
> As Sumer's people process before divine Inanna
> The Morning Lady, Inanna, shines with brightness
> And I sing out in praise of you, O heavenly Inanna
> On the horizon the Morning Lady shines brightly[2]

Her Akkadian name Ishtar means 'Lady Star', while her name Inanna means 'Queen of Heaven' in Sumerian.[3] And according to the Babylonian creation epic 'Enuma Elish' Ishtar was identified with the Bow Star, which is our constellation of *Canis Major*.[4] However, the goddess shares a broader association with the Milky Way and Moon. The Goddess's link with the Moon has something to do with the image of the 'lady reading' upon its surface when full, which in ancient times was identified as a bride: to the Greeks this moon image was known as Pandora, while in Nordic myth she was Gunnlod, guardian of the sacred Mead of Poetry (see *The Eden Enigma*). The Moon as viewed from Earth appears as other forms during its phase changes; its crescent often likened to horns, and thus associated with cows. Dumuzi's sister Geshtinanna could thus be equivalent to the 'moon cow', and is referred to as the 'wild cow' in the Akkadian version of the descent.[5]

Geshtinanna's name means "ear Inanna", which would translate more accurately into English as "wise Inanna", and thus likely by extension "moon Inanna"; but who is clearly but an aspect of the Goddess herself, specifically representing the aspect of Inanna as the Moon. And Inanna is identified as the daughter of Sin or Nanna, who is likewise the moon god. It must be that in ancient Sumer, and perhaps generally in ancient times, that the ear was believed to be the seat of intelligence, and thus the word was utilized to indicate such. Though the Moon was also widely associated with wisdom, and this could be because the half-moons appeared to them as large ears in the night sky. This is so of the Norse moon god Heimdall, who was to have been a deity with particularly acute hearing.*

---

* Likewise the Egyptian moon god Thoth is referred to as the 'hearing ear' in the Greek Magical Papyri. (PGM *Suppl.* 150; see Betz 1992: 328)

Thus the three goddesses Inanna, Geshtinanna, and Belili are all merely aspects of the same goddess; considering that Geshtinanna represents the virgin, Inanna the wife, and Belili the old hag, as such a circumstance is not without equivalent, particularly in the closely related Greek tale of Demeter and Persephone. And this is certainly the case given that Belili is merely the name for Geshtinanna in the Akkadian version of the myth, which could be '*bel-lili*' and thus would also be similar to Ninlil ('Lady Lil') and Lilith,* the latter being a devouring goddess responsible for childhood death and disease.[6] And as Demeter, the Mother Goddess, seems to have been associated with the Milky Way,[7] such might be so of Old Belili. And thus it might be that the Queen of Heaven was divided up according to this divine trinity:

Inanna/Ishtar -	Morning/Evening Star
Geshtinanna/Belili -	Moon
Old Belili -	Milky Way

But each of these goddesses is also one of cycles: of the diurnal cycle, the lunar cycle, and the celestial cycle. Although the very descent of Ishtar, who is absent for three days prior to when Ninshubur commences the ritual mourning for her, is linked to the three days in which the moon is dark in the sky, during the period of the New Moon. And thus Ereshkigal, Queen of the Underworld, might well also be a goddess of the dark moon.

The myth of Ishtar's descent into the underworld would not be as old as the concept behind it, which is an explanation of the alternation of the seasons, of the two halves of the year: summer and winter. And just as Ishtar is Queen of Heaven, her sister Ereshkigal's name means 'Queen of the Underworld'; and the motivation for Ishtar to go into the underworld in the Sumerian version is to attend the funeral of Ereshkigal's husband Gugalanna, the Bull of Heaven (slain by Gilgamesh and Enkidu in the 'Epic of Gilgamesh'), the constellation of *Taurus*. The descent of Ishtar thus commences after *Taurus* sets below the horizon at sunset in the spring (during the Age of Taurus), and shortly thereafter descends the nearby constellation of *Orion*, which was identified as Dumuzi by the ancient Babylonians;[8] whereas its re-emergence corresponds to the arrival of Dumuzi to Ishtar at harvest time when the sun was in *Scorpius*.[9]

Clearly there is a link between Ishtar and the *vernal equinox*, falling around March 21 on our calendar, and especially with the Full Moon subsequent to it. This is especially noteworthy in relation to the equivalence of the name Ishtar to that of Easter, which when adopted by the Christians only added that the day was to be celebrated on the first *Sunday* following the first Full Moon after the vernal equinox, which is how it is still determined. It likewise indicates the association of Easter with the moon goddess specifically, as both the rabbit and the egg are features visible upon its surface when the

---

* The meaning of the Sumerian word 'lil' is spirit, also wind and ghost. (Kramer 1983: 164)

moon is full. Thus we must assume that Ishtar's absence corresponds to the very period in which Geshtinanna was to have existed in the underworld in Dumuzi's place.

If Dumuzi was indeed to have been absent for half the year, during which time the land lay in desolation; and he was to have returned upon the *autumnal equinox*, falling around September 21; then it makes sense that the marriage of their youth occurred at the time of the vernal equinox.[10] Then following the youthful marriage of Ishtar with Dumuzi, her young husband was fated to meet his end not long after their nuptials. Although the actual funeral ceremony took place at the time of the summer *solstice*, around June 21, and thus he was only truly absent in the underworld for three months. This is the possible explanation as to why Dumuzi, on the run prior to being captured, visits three distinct locations: Kubiresh, the home of Old Belili, and his sister Geshtinanna's sheep farm; representing the three months of the onset of summer from vernal equinox to summer solstice. And subsequent to this there is mention within the Akkadian version of how there was raised a ritual lamentation for Dumuzi following his 'death', which marks the *etiological* initiation of the solemn *taklimtu* ceremony accompanying his statue's 'funeral' in the month of Tammuz (June/July).[11] And such is likewise recorded in the book of *Ezekiel* concerning the weeping for Tammuz (Dumuzi) in the Jerusalem temple:

> He said also unto me, Turn thee yet again, and thou shalt see greater abominations that they do. Then he brought me to the door of the gate of the LORD's house which was toward the north; and, behold, there sat women weeping for Tammuz. (*Ezekiel 8:13-14, KJV*)

Once the restoration of Dumuzi was fulfilled, and he was thus reunited with his wife, then would return the fertility of the land. And in the Sumerian festival performed every New Year at the autumnal *equinox* a *hieros gamos*, or the ritual marriage marking the return of Dumuzi and his reunion with Inanna, would be played out.[12] In this the Sumerian king would take the place of Dumuzi the shepherd: assuming his name and offering gifts to the goddess to win her favor. If he were accepted by her then the ritual marriage would take place and the sacred bed would be prepared for them; marking the time when Dumuzi was reunited with his wife, the Queen of Heaven, who was represented by the high priestess of Inanna;[13] thus making Inanna both goddess and bride, the same bride to be seen upon the face of the moon.

The descent of the Goddess into the underworld was not retained in the Biblical tradition which eventually eviscerated any trace of divinity apart from that of the single almighty god Yahweh. Thus the comprehension of the seasonal change as due to the alternation between Dumuzi and Geshtinanna in the underworld is not strictly retained

---

[*] The year was divided into two halves separated by the *equinoxes*. Dumuzi ruled over the barley that grew during the wet season, and thus also the beer; while Geshtinanna ruled over the grapes and figs that grew during the dry season. (Kramer 1983: 168)

within the Biblical tradition. But there are three tales relating to the 'gods' sharing the year between them, with one associated with the Sun and the other with the Moon; and these are the tale of Cain and Abel, and that of Jacob and Esau from the book of *Genesis*, and the story contained within the book of *Esther*. Within the story of Inanna she must choose between a shepherd and a farmer, which parallels the story of Cain and Abel, wherein it is Yahweh who is doing the choosing based upon the sacrifices made to him:

> *And Abel was a keeper of sheep, but Cain was a tiller of the ground. And in process of time it came to pass, that Cain brought of the fruit of the ground an offering unto the LORD. And Abel, he also brought of the firstlings of his flock and of the fat thereof. And the LORD had respect unto Abel and to his offering: but unto Cain and to his offering he had not respect. And Cain was very wroth, and his countenance fell.* (**Genesis 4:2-5, KJV**)

Where in this case Abel is the sun and Cain is the moon; while the confrontation between the brothers Jacob and Esau also derives from the alternation of gods, with Jacob being the moon god and associated with the constellation of *Ursa Major*, while Esau is the sun god and associated with the constellation of *Capricornus*.[14] In the book of *Esther* the Goddess appears in the person of Esther herself, which is the Hebrew equivalent of Ishtar; while Mordecai, the great Babylonian god-king Marduk,[15] and his adversary Haman once would have been god figures associated respectively with the sun and moon. This is quite distinct, however, from the conception of the alternation between Dumuzi and Geshtinanna, as the former specifically represents vegetative growth, as god of the rising barley, without a direct identification with the sun.

One must look for the closest equivalent of Ishtar's descent within the mythology of the Norse, which was not recorded in writing until the 13th century in Iceland, hundreds of years after they had officially adopted Christianity. In their poems and tales is preserved a significant amount of Nordic mythic tradition, although the emphasis within the Nordic story is upon the god figure of Balder, Odin's son and Dumuzi's equivalent, rather than Balder's wife Nanna, whose name is distinctly akin to that of Inanna, though she factors very insignificantly in the story. But both Balder and Dumuzi are known to have experienced a dream, each portending his fateful end; and as Dumuzi is ultimately betrayed by his 'friend' thus too Balder is shot down by his own blind brother Hod, god of darkness; and the weeping for Balder is clearly reflective of the mournful weeping expressed at the passing of Dumuzi on the summer solstice; and which would serve as the agency for his eventual return, as well as representing a manifest charm to bring rain. And just as with Ishtar's descent, in the Norse version Odin's son Hermod makes such a journey into the underworld of Hel. Such does the fate of Dumuzi closely match that of Balder. However, the descent of the Goddess into the depths of the underworld is a rather similar Nordic myth known as 'The Song of Odin's Ravens' which could be termed the 'Descent of Idunna'; and clearly here too there is a parallel between Idunna's name and that of Inanna. So it is likely that the same goddess made her way into the north twice, through two different mythic traditions.

As far as the provenance of the descent of Ishtar, its tablets dating back to the early 2nd millennium BC were uncovered from 1899 through the early 20th century AD by archaeologists from the heaped remains (*tells*) of the ancient cities of Nippur and Ur. From the identification, sorting, and overlaying of multiple tablets a nearly complete version of the Sumerian 'Descent of Inanna' was reclaimed, apart from a small lacuna of about 20 lines near its end; while the Akkadian 'Descent of Ishtar' is virtually complete but substantially shorter in length. Thus the presentation of the Akkadian 'Descent of Ishtar' is straightforward, while that of Inanna has been sequenced into three segments, that of 'The Wooing of Inanna', 'From the Great Above', and 'Dumuzi's Dream'.[16] The first of these amounts to segments relating to the meeting of the divine couple, while the second presents the complete story of the descent itself up to the gap. 'Dumuzi's Dream' concludes matters, with the addition of a reconstruction of the missing lines and the closing lines of 'From the Great Above'.

While it is amazing to find that the Sumerian tale might be rendered largely complete, there is still the potential that eventual archaeological work in excavating the *tells* of the Near East, which contain the remains of cities layered one upon each other through time, might promise an entirely uninterrupted version of this and other Mesopotamian myths; not to mention the potential of entirely new ones surfacing. However, the cultural treasures of ancient Mesopotamia are right now being looted and sold as collectable curiosities, and this certainly makes it a tragedy of modern times: that relics which have endured in the ground for millennia are now being sold to a market hungry for ancient artifacts to add to private collections; few of which will find their way into museums, and even if they did their provenance and most of the historical information concerning them would already have been lost. Such collectors of antiquities and 'lost treasures' do nothing to aid their preservation, but rather *further* the destructive impacts of improper excavation and the resultant loss of data which aids in identifying historical contexts, which once lost can never be reclaimed.

The two further myths included here are an entirely different kettle of fish. The 'Epic of Anzu' and 'Erra and Ishum' present two tales which deal with armed conflict, heroic conquests, and the assumption of total power. The first of these tells of the cosmic contest between a vile monster and a valiant god, which appears to have far deeper mythological roots than is apparent from a mere reading of the myth alone. The other, that of 'Erra and Ishum', is a rather idiosyncratic story; and somewhat uneven due to its enigmatic character, which is exacerbated by a significant gap in the middle of it. The tale of 'Erra and Ishum' does not rely upon a narrative development but a sequence of challenges and arguments between gods. Yet its unique approach might arise from one of two sources: an attempt to explicate the capricious nature of the gods themselves, or that the original tale was to have been conjured in a dream. And while the nature of the myth itself gives favor to the former of these, the latter is addressed in the final lines recorded upon the tablets, wherein it is stated that this myth was derived from a dream of one Kabti-ilani-Marduk, the son of Dabibi. It goes on to say that he recited the dream after waking and recounted the entirety of it; and that it was approved by Erra, Ishum, and every other of the gods; while the declaration then given by Erra which accompanies this has been included in the myth's *Epilogue*.

The 'Epic of Anzu' is the story of the god Ninurta, better known and given here as Nimrod, and his confrontation with the lion-faced thunderbird Anzu. Principally derived from the 'Standard Babylonian' version from the 1st millennium BC, certain lines of it have been borrowed from the Old Babylonian version from the early 2nd millennium BC. And just as with the creation, flood, and other mythic events, this deed is attributed to more than one god; in this case the underworld god Nergal in the tale of 'Erra and Ishum' which follows. This latter myth is believed to be from a later period, the first millennium BC, and serves a similar purpose as does the creation epic 'Enuma Elish', in that the gods are bothered by the uproar created by man. Although the chief motivator within the story is the nature of the Warlord Erra, given to wild bouts of anger and aggression in which he rages against mankind; and thus a justifiable explanation for the precarious and unpredictable fate of human existence. It was not uncommon to attribute any natural or psychological manifestation as deriving from some determinative cause, and thus a natural explanation for any consequence was to immediately attribute such a cause to it, commonly the punishment of a god for some sin committed against that god. Curiously, such a sentiment; often expressed in the ancient world for bad luck, affliction, accident, or defeat; as deriving from some personal violation is resurfacing again in the form of attributing one's fate entirely to their personal 'choices'. Perhaps it is all an attempt to gain a sense of order and justice in one's life, but at the same time it shows how little people have changed. But these myths, as all Mesopotamian myths, contain some number of gaps due to tablet fragmentation; but there is no obvious means or meaningful reason to attempt to occupy the gaps with filler and thus lacunae have been marked with a '※'.

While the 'Descent of Ishtar' stands among the many mythologies of the world which attempt to characterize the seasonal cycle as the trading-off of one deity with another for control over the earth (see *Blood and Incest*), the Mesopotamian version is unique in that it arises out of family ties and compassion rather than conflict and violence. For whereas most of the others are typically comprehended as being a contest between two brothers, as with Cain and Abel, or a father and son caught in an endless cycle of bloody confrontations, the 'Descent of Ishtar' has a sister acting in self-sacrifice to save her brother from perpetual death, thus engendering instead a cycle of endless rebirths. And in her many aspects, Ishtar was no doubt one of the most honored among the deities of ancient Mesopotamia, and not so much for her raw power as her natural dynamism: as the goddess of cyclical change and the heavens; and of life, love, death, and rebirth; which were likewise viewed as being inescapably intertwined.

THE DESCENT OF ISHTAR

It was to the kingdom of Kurnugi, the Realm of No Return,[*]
This is where Sin's daughter was intent upon going, Ishtar![†]
Sin's daughter was intent on going to the abode of darkness,
There where lives the Divine One of Erkalla, the Great City[‡]
To the abode which refuses to permit its guests to depart,
Upon the way which allows passage in only one direction
Down into the abode where every visitor is denied all light
Where the only food is dirt and where the only bread is clay
No light penetrates there; they live in a shade of darkness
The covering they wear is feathers like the plumage of birds
Where dust has gathered upon both the lock and the lintel

When she had arrived at the gate of Kurnugi, Ishtar spoke,
And addressed her words to the guardian of the gate, saying,
"You, gatekeeper! You must now open your gate before me,
Open your gate in front of me that I might pass through!
And if you fail to open this gate so that I might pass through,
Then I will break down the door, and smash its lock to bits!
I'll breach the post and bring the gate-doors crashing down
And I will shatter both of its hinges and break off the knob
Then I will cause the dead to rise to consume those that live,
So the number of the dead will be more than those that live!"
The gatekeeper opened his mouth, saying to mighty Ishtar,

---

[*] The Sumerian word Kurnugi means 'Land of No Return' and refers to the underworld.
[†] Sin (the Sumerian Nanna) is the Babylonian moon god
[‡] Erkalla means 'Great City' and refers to the underworld.

The Descent of Ishtar

"Cease, My Lady, and refrain from breaking down the door!
Rather allow me to go to Queen Ereshkigal and inform her."
So the gatekeeper proceeded within and spoke to Ereshkigal,
"She has come, Ishtar your sister, **from the realm of the sky**[*]
She who holds in her possession the mighty springing-toy
Who, when she is with Ea, agitates the waters of the Apsu."[†]
When Ereshkigal had heard, she went red as raw tamarisk,
And her lips deepened in hue like the *kuninu*-vessel's brim,
"Why has she come here? What provoked her to confront me?
It must not be because I have drunk at the Anunnaki's table,[‡]
Or not that I have clay as my bread, or dirty water as my beer
It is I who suffers tears for the youths forced to leave their loves
It is I who cries for maidens snatched from their darlings' laps
It is I who must weep for the babe who is doomed all too soon
So, guardian of the gate, go and make the way open for her,
And let her experience what the most ancient rites decree."
Thus the gate's guardian departed, opening the way for her,
"Enter, Lady. And may the land of Kutha bring you delight,[§]
And may the Realm of No Return's citadel be glad to see you!"
Thus he allowed her to pass through the door of the first gate,
But he tore off and kept the splendid crown upon her head
(And Ishtar raised her voice to be heard, to the gatekeeper,)

---

[*] Bold text is used throughout to indicate the restoration of a gap in the tablet due to damage.
[†] Ea is the Akkadian water god and ruler of the Apsu, the great watery abyss beneath the earth.
[‡] The Anunnaki are gods of the underworld
[§] Kutha is the temple of Nergal, king of the underworld, thus indicating the underworld itself.

"Why did you tear the splendid crown from off of my head?"

(And the gatekeeper raised his voice to be heard, to Ishtar,)

"Enter Lady, for these are the ways of the Mistress of Earth."*

He allowed her to pass through the door of the second gate,

But he tore off and kept the earrings which adorned her ears

(And Ishtar raised her voice to be heard, to the gatekeeper,)

"Why did you take from me the earrings adorning my ears?"

(And the gatekeeper raised his voice to be heard, to Ishtar,)

"Enter Lady, for these are the ways of the Mistress of Earth."

He allowed her to pass through the door of the third gate,

But he tore off and kept the bead necklace about her neck

(And Ishtar raised her voice to be heard, to the gatekeeper,)

"Why did you take the bead necklace from about my neck?"

(And the gatekeeper raised his voice to be heard, to Ishtar,)

"Enter Lady, for these are the ways of the Mistress of Earth."

He allowed her to pass through the door of the fourth gate,

But he tore off and kept the broach-pin clasped at her chest

(And Ishtar raised her voice to be heard, to the gatekeeper,)

"Why did you take the broach-pin clasped upon my chest?"

(And the gatekeeper raised his voice to be heard, to Ishtar,)

"Enter Lady, for these are the ways of the Mistress of Earth."

Thus he allowed her to pass through the door of the fifth gate,

But he tore off and kept the birth-stone belt girding her waist

(And Ishtar raised her voice to be heard, to the gatekeeper,)

---

* Those entering the underworld may not bring any material items with them.

"Why did you take the birth-stone belt girding my waist?"
(And the gatekeeper raised his voice to be heard, to Ishtar,)
"Enter Lady, for these are the ways of the Mistress of Earth."
Thus he allowed her to pass through the door of the sixth gate,
But he tore off and kept the bangles at her ankles and wrists
(And Ishtar raised her voice to be heard, to the gatekeeper,)
"Why did you take the bangles about my ankles and wrists?"
(And the gatekeeper raised his voice to be heard, to Ishtar,)
"Enter Lady, for these are the ways of the Mistress of Earth."
He allowed her to pass through the door of the seventh gate,
But he tore off and kept the regal garb which enwrapped her
(And Ishtar raised her voice to be heard, to the gatekeeper,)
"Why did you take the regal garb that enwrapped my body?"
(And the gatekeeper raised his voice to be heard, to Ishtar,)
"Enter, Lady, for these are the ways of the Mistress of Earth."
Just as Ishtar had descended into the Realm of No Return,
When Ereshkigal first saw her, she shivered in her presence
Ishtar did not mince words, but rather stood tall before her
Ereshkigal raised her voice, speaking to her officer, Namtar,
"Proceed now, Namtar, **who are the executor** of my **designs**,
Unleash the sixty maladies upon Ishtar, **to prevail over her**
Thus will you send the malady of the eye against her eyes,
Thus will you send the malady of the arm against her arms,
Thus will you send the malady of the foot against her feet,
Thus will you send the malady of the heart against her heart,

Thus will you send the malady of the head against her head,
Send them into every of her members and into **her very soul**."

Once Ishtar, Queen **of Heaven**, had descended into Kurnugi,
After the Goddess went down into the Realm of No Return,
Then there was not one single bull that impregnated a cow,
And there was not one single donkey that mounted a jenny,
There was not one single youth who made love to a local girl,
Rather the youth remained asleep within his own chambers,
And the girl went to bed only in the company of her close kith
Then Papsukkal, the gods' official, was low with a somber cast,
Dressed in the garments of mourning, with his hair unkempt,
Overcome with gloom, he went and cried before his father, Sin,
Standing before the great king Ea, he wept tears without end,
"Lady Ishtar has descended into the Earth, and not returned
Once Ishtar, Mistress of Heaven, had descended into Kurnugi,
After the Goddess went down into the Realm of No Return,
Then there was not one single bull that impregnated a cow,
And there was not one single donkey that mounted a jenny,
There was not one single youth who made love to a local girl,
Rather the youth remained asleep within his own chambers,
And the girl went to bed only in the company of her close kith."
Drawing upon the wisdom within him, Ea produced a being,

The Descent of Ishtar

Making a creation, who was a Bright Boy named Handsome.[*]

(Ea raised his voice to be heard, speaking to the Bright Boy,)

"Now, Handsome, make your way to the gates of Kurnugi,

And every one of Kurnugi's seven gates will be open for you

And when Ereshkigal sees you she will be greatly pleased,

So that she is no longer anxious and will become cheerful

Then you must make her swear an oath by Heaven's gods,

Then look aloft and take notice of the hanging water-skin,

And you will say to her, 'May I ask, Lady, that this water-skin

Be passed over to me that I might quench my thirst with it.'"

(Thus Handsome set out on his way to the gates of Kurnugi,)

(And every one of Kurnugi's seven gates did open for him)

(And when Ereshkigal gazed at him she was greatly pleased,)

(Such that she was no longer anxious and became cheerful)

(And he caused her to swear an oath by the gods of Heaven,)

(That she promise to give him anything he might request)

(So he looked aloft and took notice of the hanging water-skin,)

(And he said to her, "May I ask, Lady, that this water-skin)

(Be passed over to me that I might quench my thirst with it.")

But when Ereshkigal heard his words, she slapped her thigh,

And held her finger in her teeth, and gave her reply, saying,

"This request to me is one that you should never have made!

Thus, Handsome, I will condemn you with the worst of curses,

---

[*] Handsome is protected and can freely come and go from the underworld according to his nature of 'bright boy', which implies he is sexless. (Dalley 2000: 161)

For you I will declare a fate which will forever be remembered
Bread discarded by the city's bakers is all that you shall eat,
Water from the city's gutters is the only place you will drink,
Porch steps will be the only place you'll have to seat yourself,
Both the drunk and the wanting will strike you in the face."
Ereshkigal raised her voice, speaking to her officer, Namtar,
"Go forth, Namtar, rap on the door of the palace Everlasting,[*]
When there place corals upon the front steps to adorn them,
Have the Anunnaki come out and sit upon thrones of gold,
Shower upon Ishtar the Water of Life, and bring her to me."
So Namtar went, rapped on the door of the palace Everlasting,
And there placed corals upon the front steps to adorn them,
He had the Anunnaki come out and sit upon thrones of gold,
Showered upon Ishtar the Water of Life, and took her to her

Then he allowed her to pass through the door of the first gate,
And returned to her the regal garb meant to enwrap her body
Then allowed her to pass through the door of the second gate,
And returned to her the bangles for her ankles and her wrists
Then he allowed her to pass through the door of the third gate,
And he returned to her the birth-stone belt to gird her waist
Then allowed her to pass through the door of the fourth gate,
And returned to her the broach-pin to clasp upon her chest
Then he allowed her to pass through the door of the fifth gate,

---

[*] The palace Egalgina, in the underworld

The Descent of Ishtar

And returned to her the bead necklace to hang about her neck
Then he allowed her to pass through the door of the sixth gate,
And he returned to her the earrings that would adorn her ears
Then allowed her to pass through the door of the seventh gate,
And he returned to her the splendid crown to adorn her head
(Ereshkigal raised her voice, speaking to her officer, Namtar,)
"Swear that she has paid her ransom, to be swapped for him,
For Dumuzi, her first husband when she was but a maiden,
Wash him in unsullied water, anoint him with purified oil,
Wrap him in a scarlet robe, play upon the *lapis lazuli* flute,
The ritual virgins will raise a cry of mourning for the dead."
Belili[*] ripped off her adornments, her lap strewn with gems,
As Belili heard the mourning wail in the name of her brother
She tore from off of her all the ornaments that adorned her,
All the gemstones which decorated the front of the wild cow
(Then Belili raised her voice to be heard, speaking a pledge,)
"Lo, you will not deprive me of my dear brother for all time!
For upon that day to come, when Dumuzi once more arises,
And the *lapis lazuli* rod and *carnelian* ring arise with him,
And those who lament, both men and women, arise with him,
Upon that day the dead will arise to savor the smoke-offering
And then will every land be in jubilation at his awakening
But until that day comes I will ceaselessly lament for him!"
And Belili walked the city, weeping for Dumuzi, her brother.

---

[*] Also called Geshtinanna, Dumuzi's sister

THE DESCENT OF INANNA

THE WOOING OF INANNA

The brother was speaking to his little sister,
Utu, the Sun God, said as he spoke to Inanna,
"Young lady, all the ripe flax is enchanting
Inanna, all the grain is resplendent in the fields
So I will reap it for you, and carry it to you
There is always need for linen, large or small
So then Inanna, I will carry all of it to you."
Inanna, the Queen of Heaven, spoke to Utu,
"But brother when you bring me the flax,
Who will be the one who combs it for me?"
Utu, the Sun God, speaking to Inanna, said,
"Sister, I will be the one who will comb it."
Inanna, the Queen of Heaven, spoke to Utu,
"But Utu, after you have provided it combed,
Who will be the one who spins it for me?"
Utu, the Sun God, speaking to Inanna, said,
"Inanna, I will be the one who spins it for you."
Inanna, the Queen of Heaven, spoke to Utu,
"Brother, after you have provided spun flax,
Who will be the one who braids it for me?"
Utu, the Sun God, speaking to Inanna, said,
"Sister, I will be the one who braids it for you."

13

The Descent of Inanna

Inanna, the Queen of Heaven, spoke to Utu,
"But Utu, after you have provided it braded,
Who will be the one who warps it for me?"
Utu, the Sun God, speaking to Inanna, said,
"Inanna, I'll be the one who warps it for you."
Inanna, the Queen of Heaven, spoke to Utu,
"Brother, after you have provided it warped,
Who will be the one who weaves it for me?"
Utu, the Sun God, speaking to Inanna, said,
"Sister, I'll be the one who weaves it for you."
Inanna, the Queen of Heaven, spoke to Utu,
"But Utu, after you have provided it woven,
Who will be the one who bleaches it for me?"
Utu, the Sun God, speaking to Inanna, said,
"Inanna, I'll be the one who bleaches it for you."
Inanna, the Queen of Heaven, spoke to Utu,
"But brother, once you've given a sheet to me,
Who will then come with me to my bridal bed?
Utu, who will lie beside me in the bridal bed?"
Utu, the Sun God, speaking to Inanna, said,
"Sister, you will share your bed with the groom
It is he who emerged from the fruitful womb
He was conceived upon the holy marriage bed
The shepherd, Dumuzi, will come to your bed."
Inanna, the Queen of Heaven, spoke to Utu,

"He is not, brother, the man who stole my heart,
Rather it is the farmer, him who plies the hoe,
He is the gentleman who has stolen my heart!
For he collects together immense heaps of grain
And seasonally brings corn into my storerooms."
Utu, the Sun God, speaking to Inanna, said,
"Sister, take the shepherd, why would you not?
After all he has delicious cream, sweet milk,
And what he touches shines like the heavens
So Inanna, marry Dumuzi, why would you not?
Having bedecked yourself with rich necklaces
Dumuzi will deliver his richest cream to you
You who are allotted to be the king's guardian
So Inanna, marry Dumuzi, why would you not?"
Inanna, the Queen of Heaven, spoke to Utu,
"Why the shepherd? I refuse to marry him!
For he has only coarse fabrics, rough wool,
Rather, Utu, I would wish to marry the farmer,
For the farmer will grow flax fit for my robes
And the farmer will grow barley for my fare."

Then Dumuzi, the shepherd, spoke to Inanna,
"There is no reason for you to praise the farmer,
Why do you insist upon speaking about him?
For if he provides black flour, I will black wool

15

The Descent of Inanna

If he provides you white flour, I will white wool
If he provides you beer, I will give sweet milk
If he provides you bread, I'll give honey cheese
The farmer only receives my surplus of cream
The farmer only receives my surpluses of milk
So why do you go on talking about the farmer?
Are his possessions more abundant than mine?"
Inanna, Queen of Heaven, spoke to Dumuzi,
"Shepherd, but for Ningal you would be gone
But for Ningikuga, you would live in the hills
If not for Nanna, you'd have no roof over you[*]
And if it were not to for my brother, Utu..."
Then Dumuzi, the shepherd, interrupted her,
"Inanna, do not think to provoke a squabble,
For my father Enki is as noble as your father
And my mother Sirtur as noble as your mother
And my sister, Geshtinanna, as noble as yours
So rather, Queen of the Citadel, we should talk,
Rather Inanna, we ought to meet and converse
As I am noble as Utu; so too Enki is as Nanna[†]
So rather, Queen of the Citadel, we should talk."
The words they spoke were filled with longing
Their clash, from the first, had spurred on love

---

[*] Ningal ('Queen') is Inanna's mother, Ningikuga her grandmother, Nanna her father
[†] The Sumerian god Enki is god of water and equivalent to the Akkadian god Ea. The Sumerian god Nanna is god of the moon and equivalent to the Akkadian god Sin.

So the shepherd came to the palace with cream
Dumuzi came to the citadel carrying sweet milk
When standing before the door, he called to her,
"Open up your house, my dear; open the door!"
Inanna ran to her mother Ningal, who bore her,
Ningal gave advice to her daughter, and said,
"My child, the young man will be like a father
Daughter, to you he will also be like a mother
You will find him treating you as if your father
And find him caring for you as if your mother
Open up your house, my dear; open the door!"
So Inanna went, just as her mother directed her,
She washed herself, anointed herself with oil,
Draped her body with the finest of white robes
Set forth her dowry, lay beads about her neck
Taking up the royal emblem into her deft hand
While Dumuzi waited for her arrival impatiently
Before Inanna opened wide the door for him
And within the house she was readily beaming
Holding the bewitching aura of the Full Moon
Dumuzi was overcome with delight as he gazed
Then moving even closer to her, he kissed her.

Then she sought it, she sought for it
She sought after it, sought after it, she sought the bed

The Descent of Inanna

She sought the bed which brings elation to the heart
She sought for the bed which brings delight to the lap
She sought the kingly bed, she sought the queenly bed
Thus Inanna sought after the bed,
"May the bed that brings the heart joy be made ready!
May the bed that brings the lap delight be made ready!
Let the kingly bed be made ready
Let the queenly bed be made ready
Let the regal bed be made ready!"
And Inanna spread the honeymoon sheet upon the bed
She told the king, "The bed is prepared!"
She told the groom, "The bed is ready!"

Then he touched his hand to her hand,
And he touched his hand to her heart
Such delight comes from the sleep of hands touching,
More delight comes from the sleep of hearts touching
Inanna said, "I laved for the buffalo bull
I laved myself for Dumuzi, the shepherd
I spread aromatic oil upon my shapeliness
I drenched my mouth with fragrant butter
I decorated my eyes with dark *kohl* powder
He fondled my genitals with sweet hands
The shepherd Dumuzi poured milk and cream in my lap
Caressed my fine bush, doused my womb,

His hands did fondle my blessed genitals,
With cream he plied my dark boat evenly
With milk made my slender craft speedy
He touched me with softness upon the bed
I will stroke my high priest upon the bed
I will stroke the devoted shepherd Dumuzi
I will stroke the lap of the land's shepherd
And declare for him a favorable destiny."
Thus did the Lady of Heaven, valiant lady;
Who outshines her mother, received the Arts from Enki;
The eldest daughter of the Moon, Inanna,
Declare a favorable destiny for Dumuzi:
"In times of war I do marshal your forces
Within the skirmish I carry your armor,
At the gathering I speak to your benefit,
On the warpath I inspire steady insight
Chosen shepherd of the sanctified shrine,
You king, Uruk's steadfast bearer of gifts,
You who illumine the great temple of An,*
According to any measure you are perfect
To raise up your head upon the high stage
To seat yourself on the *lapis lazuli* throne
To place on your head the sacred diadem
To wear long robes, and bind the royal sash about you

---

* An is the Sumerian sky god, called Anu in Akkadian.

The Descent of Inanna

To hold in your hands the sword and mace
To make true the bow and arrow's path
To bind the club and sling upon your belt
To charge upon the path, brandishing the sacred scepter
Wearing upon your feet the sacred sandals
To parade upon the sacred ground like a *lapis lazuli* calf
You, O chosen shepherd, are the fleet one
According to any measure you are perfect
May your soul be blessed with long life
Let that which An has chosen for you never be retracted
Let that which Enlil provided to you never be withdrawn[*]
You, beloved of Ningal; Inanna's dearest."

The dedicated deaconess of Uruk's temple, Ninshubur,
Guided Dumuzi to Inanna's delightful thighs and said,
"O Queen, here is your heart's favorite,
Here is the king, your cherished groom
May he for long hours find delight in your blessed lap!
Grant him a long and magnificent reign
Give him the king's throne, firmly set,
Give him the shepherd's staff of rule,
Give the headdress of everlastingness,
Bearing the shining imperial coronet
And from the span of sunrise to sunset,

---

[*] Enlil is the Sumerian god of the atmosphere, called Ellil in Akkadian.

North to the south, high sea to low sea,

The lands of the *huluppu* to the cedar,

May the shepherd's crook shield all Akkad and Sumer!

As cultivator, may he cause the fields to be abundant!

As shepherd, may he make the sheep farms burgeon!

As long as he reigns, may there always be green growth

As long as he reigns, may there always be plentiful grain

And within the marsh let the fish and fowl be lively

And within the reed bed let reeds of all ages rise tall

And upon the prairie, let the *mushgur* tree rise loftily

And within the wood, let deer and wild goats abound

And within the vineyard, let there be wine and honey

And within the garden, let the lettuce and kale flourish

In the royal house, let life be long,

Let there be alluvial soil within the Tigris and Euphrates

Let the foliage thrive on its banks,

And abound too within the meadow

Might the Lady of Leaves amass grain in great profusion

O my Lady of Heaven and Earth,

And queen of the entire Universe,

May he for long hours find delight in your blessed lap!

Thus the king went with head upheld to the blessed lap

Went with head upheld to the Queen

He spread broadly his arms for Heaven's high priestess

The Descent of Inanna

Inanna said, "My lover, the apple of my eye came to me
And we found our pleasure together
And I was greatly favored in his eyes
And he brought me within his house
And spread me upon the sweet-scented honeymoon bed
My darling lover, close to my heart
Thrusting tongue play, one at a time
Fifty of them did sweet Dumuzi do
Now my invigorated love is satisfied
While he says, 'Let me go, O my sister, please let me go!
You are now my father's little daughter
But now my cherished sister, let me go,
For I desire to get away to the palace!'"

Then Inanna said, "My source of the sweetest blossoms,
How thoughtfully do you enrapture!
My source of the sweetest blossoms in the apple grove,
My source of fruit in the apple grove,
O wise Dumuzi, how thoughtfully do you enrapture!
My brave one, my worshipped idol,
My idol equipped with rapier and *lapis lazuli* crown,
How thoughtfully do you enrapture!"

FROM THE GREAT ABOVE

From the vast Heaven she turned her attention to the vast Depths
From the vast Heaven the goddess contemplated the vast Depths
From the vast Heaven Inanna thought instead of the vast Depths
The Lady forsook both Heaven and Earth to go to the Underworld
Lady Inanna forsook Heaven and Earth to go to the Underworld
She forsook her place as sacred priestess to go to the Underworld
In Uruk, forsook her temple so she could go to the Underworld
In Badtibira, forsook her temple to go down to the Underworld
In Zabalam, forsook her temple to go down to the Underworld
Within Adab, forsook her temple to go down to the Underworld
Within Nippur, forsook her temple to go down to the Underworld
Within Kish, forsook her temple to go down to the Underworld
Within Akkad, forsook her temple to go down to the Underworld
She collected the seven Arts, gathering them within her hands
With the Arts now with her she began to make herself ready:
Setting the prairie tiara, the *shugurra*, on the crown of her head
And upon her forehead she composed the dangling dark curls,
Then about her neck she clasped the gracile *lapis lazuli* beads,
Allowed the twin-stranded necklace to drape upon her breast,
Then enriched her body by enwrapping it in the imperial robe,
She painted around her eyes with the cosmetic 'May He Come',
Clasping about her chest the breastplate 'May the Man Arrive',

The Descent of Inanna

Slipping on her wrist the golden bracelet,

Then grasped within her hand the *lapis lazuli* measure and cord

Then Inanna proceeded to the underworld,

Her loyal serving girl, Ninshubur, with her

Inanna addressed her words to her, saying,

"Ninshubur, my reliable aide, my supporter

My source of sage words, my battle partner who fights at my side

I am going to the land of Kur, descending into the Underworld[*]

If I fail to return, initiate lamentations at the ruins in my name

In the meeting chamber beat the drum for me

Go in procession around the gods' temples,

Fingers scathing your eyes, mouth, and thighs,

Wearing the plain single mantle of a beggar

Travel to Nippur and enter the temple of Enlil

As you go into his sanctified temple speak thus for him to hear:

'Father Enlil, assure your daughter not die in the Underworld

Let not your shining silver be dulled by the Underworld's dust,

Your valuable *lapis lazuli* smashed to bits for the stone-worker,

Your aromatic boxwood broken into lumber for the carpenter

Don't let the divine priestess of Heaven die in the Underworld.'

But if Enlil refuses you help, then proceed on to the city of Ur

There go to Nanna's temple, and weep tears before father Nanna

As you go into his sanctified temple speak thus for him to hear:

'Father Nanna, assure your daughter not die in the Underworld

---

[*] Kur is literally 'the unknown', the land from which none return.

Let not your shining silver be dulled by the Underworld's dust,
Your valuable *lapis lazuli* smashed to bits for the stone-worker,
Your aromatic boxwood broken into lumber for the carpenter
Don't let the divine priestess of Heaven die in the Underworld.'
But if Nanna refuses you help, then proceed to the city of Eridu
There go into Enki's temple, and weep tears before father Enki
As you go into his sanctified temple speak thus for him to hear:
'Father Enki, assure your daughter not die in the Underworld
Let not your shining silver be dulled by the Underworld's dust,
Your valuable *lapis lazuli* smashed to bits for the stone-worker,
Your aromatic boxwood broken into lumber for the carpenter
Don't let the divine priestess of Heaven die in the Underworld.'
Father Enki, god of wisdom, has knowledge of the Food of Life
He has knowledge of the Water of Life, and knows the mysteries
Certainly he would not permit me to perish in the Underworld."
Thus Inanna proceeded on her journey down to the Underworld
But she hesitated for a moment and spoke to Ninshubur, saying,
"Now go, Ninshubur, and remember the words I have given you."

When Inanna reached the outermost gates of the Underworld
She knocked with firmness, speaking out in an unrelenting tone,
"Gatekeeper, you must open this door!
Hear me Neti, you must open this door!
There are none others accompanying me
For I will come through the gates alone."

The Descent of Inanna

The chief gatekeeper of Kur, Neti, queried, "Who goes there?"
She replied, "Inanna, the Lady of Heaven, headed for the east!"
Neti raised his voice and replied to her,
"If you are truly Inanna, the Lady of Heaven, going to the east,
Why do you travel upon the path from which none ever return?"
Inanna said in reply, "It has to do with Ereshkigal, my elder sister
For Gugulanna, her husband, the Bull of Heaven, has met death
And I have made the journey here to be present at his funeral
May the beer at his funeral rites be poured within the cup, Amen."
Then Neti spoke, "Then wait here, Inanna,
I will convey this to My Lady, and pass on your message to her."
Kur's head gatekeeper, Neti, proceeded into Ereshkigal's palace
Raising his voice to speak to the Lady of the Underworld, he said,
"My Lady, standing outside the gates of your palace is a maiden
She is statuesque like the heavenly sky, buxom as the earthly hills
With a fortitude matched only by the foundation of a city wall
She collected the seven Arts, gathering them into her hands
With the Arts then with her she began to make herself ready:
Setting the prairie tiara, the *shugurra*, on the crown of her head,
And upon her forehead she composed the dangling dark curls,
Then about her neck she clasped the gracile *lapis lazuli* beads,
Allowed the twin-stranded necklace to drape upon her breast,
Then enriched her body by enwrapping it in the imperial robe,
She painted around her eyes with the cosmetic 'May He Come',
Clasping about her chest the breastplate 'May the Man Arrive',

Slipping on her wrist the golden bracelet,
Then grasped within her hand the *lapis lazuli* measure and cord."
And after Ereshkigal had heard everything he had spoken to her,
At once biting her lip and slapping her hands against her thighs,
Pondered the matter deeply and considered it carefully, saying,
"Now listen to me Neti, you who act as my chief gatekeeper of Kur
You will do this: lock every one of the Underworld's seven gates
Then open each one of them in turn, but open it only just a crack
Allow Inanna to come in, but as she does take of her royal finery
Make it so that the divine priestess of Heaven comes in humility!"
And Neti listened to and sought to obey his queen's commands
And thus he locked every one of the Underworld's seven gates
Opening the first gate, he said to the girl, "You may enter, Inanna."
She proceeded forward, but as she passed through the first gate
He forcefully took from her head the prairie tiara, the *shugurra*
Inanna asked him, "What are you doing?"
And he replied to her, "Speak not, Inanna!
The Underworld's practices are faultless
You must never think to question them!"
(Opening the second gate, he said to her, "You may enter, Inanna.")
She proceeded forward, but as she passed through the second gate
He took from her neck the *lapis lazuli* beads
Inanna asked him, "What are you doing?"
And he replied to her, "Speak not, Inanna!
The Underworld's practices are faultless

You must never think to question them!"
(Opening the third gate, he said to her, "You may enter, Inanna.")
She proceeded forward, but as she passed through the third gate
He snatched from her breast the twin-stranded necklace of beads
Inanna asked him, "What are you doing?"
And he replied to her, "Speak not, Inanna!
The Underworld's practices are faultless
You must never think to question them!"
(Opening the fourth gate, he said to her, "You may enter, Inanna.")
She proceeded forward, but as she passed through the fourth gate
He tore from her chest the armor breastplate 'May the Man Arrive'
Inanna asked him, "What are you doing?"
And he replied to her, "Speak not, Inanna!
The Underworld's practices are faultless
You must never think to question them!"
(Opening the fifth gate, he said to her, "You may enter, Inanna.")
She proceeded forward, but as she passed through the fifth gate
He savagely stripped the golden bracelet from off of her wrist
Inanna asked him, "What are you doing?"
And he replied to her, "Speak not, Inanna!
The Underworld's practices are faultless
You must never think to question them!"
(Opening the sixth gate, he said to her, "You may enter, Inanna.")
She proceeded forward, but as she passed through the sixth gate
He snatched from her hand the *lapis lazuli* standard and cord

Inanna asked him, "What are you doing?"
And he replied to her, "Speak not, Inanna!
The Underworld's practices are faultless
You must never think to question them!"
(Opening the seventh gate, he said, "You may enter, Inanna.")
She proceeded, but as she passed through the seventh gate
He hotly grabbed and tore the imperial robe from off her body
Inanna asked him, "What are you doing?"
And he replied to her, "Speak not, Inanna!
The Underworld's practices are faultless
You must never think to question them!"
Now both bare naked and humiliated,
Inanna thus entered the throne room
And Ereshkigal arose from her throne
Then when Inanna took a step forward, moving to the throne,
The Annuna, the Underworld's judges
First encircled her, and then judged her
Ereshkigal fixed to Inanna the Death Eye
So too she pronounced the Word of Doom
She made against her the declaration of Guilt, and then beat her
Thus Inanna's form became a listless carcass, a slab of rancid flesh
This was then taken and fastened to hang on a hook upon the wall

When three days and nights passed and Inanna had not returned
Then Ninshubur initiated lamentations at the ruins in her name,

The Descent of Inanna

In the meeting hall she beat the drum for her,
Went in procession around the gods' temples,
Fingers scathing her eyes, mouth, and thighs,
Wearing the plain single mantle of a beggar
Then by herself she travelled to Nipur, and into Enlil's temple
Once she was inside his sanctified temple, she spoke to him thus:
"Father Enlil, assure your daughter not die in the Underworld
Let not your shining silver be dulled by the Underworld's dust,
Your valuable *lapis lazuli* smashed to bits for the stone-worker,
Your aromatic boxwood broken into lumber for the carpenter
Don't let the divine priestess of Heaven die in the Underworld."
And the patriarch Enlil replied with ire:
"First my daughter desired vast Heaven
Then my daughter desired vast Depths
Anyone who accepts the Arts of the Underworld never returns
The one entering the Dark City remains."
Thus the patriarch Enlil refused her aid
Then Ninshubur proceeded to Ur, and into Nanna's holy shrine
Once she was inside his sanctified temple, she spoke to him thus:
"Father Nanna, assure your daughter not die in the Underworld
Let not your shining silver be dulled by the Underworld's dust,
Your valuable *lapis lazuli* smashed to bits for the stone-worker,
Your aromatic boxwood broken into lumber for the carpenter
Don't let the divine priestess of Heaven die in the Underworld."
And the patriarch Nanna replied with ire:

"First my daughter desired vast Heaven

Then my daughter desired vast Depths

Anyone who accepts the Arts of the Underworld never returns

The one entering the Dark City remains."

Thus the patriarch Nanna refused her aid

Then Ninshubur proceeded on to Eridu, into Enki's holy shrine

Once she was inside his sanctified temple, she spoke to him thus:

"Father Enki, assure your daughter not die in the Underworld

Let not your shining silver be dulled by the Underworld's dust,

Your valuable *lapis lazuli* smashed to bits for the stone-worker,

Your aromatic boxwood broken into lumber for the carpenter

Don't let the divine priestess of Heaven die in the Underworld."

Father Enki said, "What took place, what did my daughter do?

Lady Inanna, Queen of the World, and holy Mistress of Heaven,

What took place, it disturbs me? I am deeply distressed by this."

And he drew an extraction of mud from beneath his fingernail

Forming this mud into a Kurgarra, a being not male or female[*]

He drew an extraction of mud from the nail of his other hand

Forming this mud into a Galatur, a being not male or female

To the Kurgarra he handed the Food of Life

To the Galatur he handed the Water of Life

Enki raised his voice, to the Kurgarra and the Galatur, saying,

"Descend into the Underworld, slip into the door as a fly would

---

[*] This is apparently a key attribute for being able to transgress the boundary of the underworld and return.

The Descent of Inanna

You will find the Lady of the Underworld, Ereshkigal, soughing
She will do so with the outbursts of a woman who is giving birth
There will be no linen garment upon her, her breasts will be bare
Her hair will be disheveled, twirling about her head like leeks
When you hear her sigh, 'oh my insides', repeat, 'oh my insides'
When you hear her sigh, 'oh my outside', repeat, 'oh my outside'
When she hears this the queen will be cheered, and offer a gift
Request only the carcass which hangs on a hook upon the wall
One will sprinkle it with the Food of Life
The other will do so with the Water of Life
And then Inanna will rise up."

The Kurgarra and the Galatur acted upon what Enki had said
They journeyed to the Underworld,
Both slipping through the gap in the gate just as a fly would do
And they entered the throne room of the Lady of the Underworld
There was no linen garment covering her, her breasts were bare
And her hair was disheveled, twirling about her head like leeks
Ereshkigal sighed, "oh my insides"; they sighed, "oh my insides"
When she sighed, "oh my outside"; they sighed, "oh my outside"
Then Ereshkigal ceased for a time and gazed at the two of them
Then she asked of them, "Who might you be? Who sigh with me,
And moan and groan? If you are divine I will give you a blessing
While if you are mortal beings then I will bestow unto you a gift
I would give you the Water Gift, which is the river's abundance."

The Kurgarra and Galatur replied, "It is not what we would like."
Ereshkigal said, "Then I will give you the Barley Gift, of rich fields."
The Kurgarra and Galatur replied, "It is not what we would like."
Ereshkigal answered, "Then tell me what you would wish to have?"
And they replied, "We want only the carcass hanging on the wall."
And Ereshkigal answered, "That carcass is the property of Inanna."
They replied, "Whether it be a queen's or king's we would like it."
And thus they received the carcass
And the Kurgarra took the Food of Life and sprinkled it upon it
And the Galatur took the Water of Life and sprinkled it upon it
And then Inanna rose up...

Inanna was to rise from the Underworld
When the Underworld judges, the Annuna, grabbed hold of her
And they told her, "None rise from the Underworld unscathed
If you wish to go from the Underworld
You must offer another in your place."
So then, as Inanna arose from the depths of the Underworld,
The Underworld's *galla*-demons remained tight around her
These *galla*-demons neither eat any food, nor take any drink,
Nor consume the offerings, nor partake of the holy libations
They received no gifts, nor delight in the pleasures of love
And they haven't any adorable children that they might kiss
Rather they take the wife out of the arms of her husband
The child from its father's lap, the bride from her new home

The Descent of Inanna

Thus the demons remained tightly bound around Inanna

The short *galla* with her like reeds as low as the lowest fence

The tall *galla* with her like reeds as high as the highest fence

The one before Inanna carried a staff, but was not a priest

The one behind Inanna had a mace, but was not a warlord

Ninshubur was standing out near the gateway to the palace

Dressed in a sullied robe made of sackcloth[*]

Upon seeing Inanna encircled by the *galla*

She bowed down to the ground at her feet

The *galla*-demons told her, "You may go to your city, Inanna,

We would be satisfied to take Ninshubur as your replacement."

And Inanna spoke passionately to them, "Do not take her!

Ninshubur is my reliable aide, my supporter,

My source of sage words, my partner who fights at my side

And she did not forget what I had told her

She made laments at the ruins in my name

In the meeting hall she beat the drum for me,

Went in procession around the gods' temples,

Fingers scathing her eyes, mouth, and thighs,

Wearing the plain single mantle of a beggar

By herself she made her way to the temple of Enlil in Nippur,

And travelled to the temple of Nanna in Ur,

And travelled to the temple of Enki in Eridu

---

[*] Indicating that Ninshubur has been in mourning

Thus she was responsible for saving my life
Thus I will never let you take Ninshubur!"
The *galla* said, "Proceed Inanna, as we go with you to Umma."
Within the temple in Umma they found Inanna's son, Shara,
Dressed in a sullied robe made of sackcloth
Upon seeing Inanna encircled by the *galla*,
He bowed down to the ground at her feet
The *galla*-demons told her, "You may go to your city, Inanna,
For we would be satisfied to take Shara, your son, in your place."
Inanna spoke passionately, "No, do not take Shara, my son!
For he sings hymns for me, and trims and brushes my hair
No, I will not allow you to take Shara!"
The *galla* said, "Proceed Inanna, as we go with you to Badtibira."
Within the temple in Badtibira they found Inanna's son, Lulal,
Dressed in a sullied robe made of sackcloth
Upon seeing Inanna encircled by the *galla*,
He bowed down to the ground at her feet
The *galla*-demons told her, "You may go to your city, Inanna,
For we would be satisfied to take Lulal, your son, in your place."
Inanna spoke passionately, "No, do not take Lulal, my son!
For he is a great leader of men, my right arm and my left arm
No, I will not allow you to take Lulal!"
So the *galla* said to her, "Then proceed on Inanna to your city,
And we will go with you to the big apple tree standing in Uruk."
At Uruk's big apple tree they found Inanna's husband, Dumuzi,

35

The Descent of Inanna

In his gleaming robes of the divine Arts
And rigid upon his splendiferous throne
The *galla*-demons grabbed him by his legs
They overturned his seven churns so that the milk spilled out
They snapped in two the shepherd's reed pipe he was playing
Inanna fixed upon Dumuzi the Death Eye
So too she pronounced the Word of Doom
She made against him a declaration of Guilt:
"Now grab him, and take Dumuzi far away!"
These *galla* who neither eat any food, nor take any drink,
Nor consume the offerings, nor partake of the holy libations,
And who receive no gifts, captured Dumuzi
They forced him to stand up and they forced him to sit down
They pummeled Inanna's husband, slashed him with blades
And Dumuzi lifted up his arms to Heaven
And to Utu, the god of justice, he implored:
"Utu, my brother-in-law, I married your sister
I delivered the cream to your mother's place
And I delivered the milk to Ningal's place
It was I who brought the meal into the temple
It was I who carried nuptial gifts to Uruk
(It was I who kissed upon those blessed lips)
It was I who sported on the sacred knees, Inanna's knees!
O Utu, god of uprightness and of boundless compassion,
Alter my hands that they become like those of a serpent

And alter my feet that they become like those of a serpent
Set me free from my demons, and do not let them take me!"
And the compassionate Utu was guided by Dumuzi's plea
Thus he altered his hands to become like those of a serpent
So too he altered his feet to become like those of a serpent
Dumuzi escaped from his demons; they could not keep him.

DUMUZI'S DREAM

His heart was overwhelmed with tears
The shepherd's heart was full of tears
The heart of Dumuzi was full of tears
Shambling on the prairie, Dumuzi cried,
"O prairie, raise a lament in my name
O crabs within the creek, grieve for me
O frogs of the stream, croak out for me
O Sirtur, who gave me birth, cry for me
If the five beads have escaped her notice,
If the ten beads have escaped her notice,
If she lacks knowledge of the day I died,
Then you, O prairie, inform my mother
Upon the open prairie my mother will shed tears for me
Upon the prairie my little sister will lift a lament for me."
Then he settled down to rest himself
The shepherd lay down to rest himself
Dumuzi settled down to rest himself
Sleeping among the lilies and reeds
And there he did experience a dream
And he awoke after he had his dream
He shivered from what he had seen,
And covered his eyes in great dread

Dumuzi then spoke, and cried aloud,

"Call out, call for her, call for my sister!

My scribe, who is aware of many stories

My singer, who is aware of many songs

My sister, who knows what words mean

My seer, who knows what dreams mean

I have to converse with her, and relate to her my dream!"

Dumuzi speaking to Geshtinanna, said,

"It was a dream! Sister, hear my dream:

The reeds grow rampant around me

Rising up thickly as a forest about me

One solitary reed stalk shakes for me

From a twin-stalk one is pulled out, followed by the other

Within a grove the terribly tall trees climb all around me

My sacred hearth is doused with water

And the base of my churn falls down

My drinking cup drops from its hook

My shepherd's crook cannot be found

An eagle grabs a lamb from the sheep pen

A falcon snatches a sparrow on the fence

O sister, your goats' *lapis lazuli* beards do touch the ground

Your sheep paw at the dirt with bent hoof

Idle sits the churn, unfilled the milk urn,

The cup is broken, Dumuzi is forsaken,

And the sheep farm is lost to the winds."

The Descent of Inanna

Geshtinanna then gave her reply, saying,
"Brother, this dream of yours should not be revealed to me!
Dumuzi, such a dream as this should not be revealed to me!
For the reeds which did grow about you,
The reeds like a forest rising around you,
These are your demons, who will come for you to assail you
The one solitary reed that shakes for you,
That is our mother, who will wail for you
The twin-stalked reed, where one is pulled
Followed by the other, Dumuzi, signifies us;
For first one and then the other will be taken
And within the grove the terribly tall trees
Climbing about you, represent *galla* demons
Who will fall upon you on the sheep farm
And when the fire upon your sacred hearth is extinguished,
Then the sheep farm will become barren
When the base of your churn does fall,
Then you will be captured by the *galla*
When your cup drops from off its hook,
So will you drop down to earth, falling into your mother's lap
When your shepherd's crook vanished,
The *galla* will make all things shrivel up
And the eagle that grabs a lamb from out of the sheep pen,
This is the *galla*, who will slash your cheeks
And the falcon that snatches a sparrow from off of the fence,

This is the *galla*, who will come over the fence to capture you

O Dumuzi, as my goats' *lapis lazuli* beards touch the ground,

So too will my hair twirl in the sky for you!

As my sheep paw at the dirt with bent hoof,

O Dumuzi, so too will I scratch my cheeks in sorrow for you!

Idle sits the churn, unfilled the milk urn,

The cup is broken, Dumuzi is forsaken,

And the sheep farm is lost to the winds."

She had hardly finished these words when Dumuzi called,

"Sister, climb up the hill with all speed,

Yet do not wander with a regal tread,

But run sister, for the *galla* are here!

Both cursed and dreaded by humanity,

They are arriving now within the boats

With them is wood to bind the hands,

With them is wood to clamp the neck; so sister, run swiftly!"

Geshtinanna ran up the side of the hill,

With her went the friend of Dumuzi

And Dumuzi called, "See them yet?"

His friend said, "They're on their way!

The short *galla* carrying with them wood to bind the hands

The tall *galla* carrying with them wood to clamp the neck

They are on their way to capture you!"

And Geshtinanna cried out, "Brother!

The Descent of Inanna

Swiftly, drop your head into the grass,
Your demons are on their way for you!"
Dumuzi then spoke to them, saying,
"O my sister, please do not reveal to anyone my hiding place
O my friend, please do not reveal to anyone my hiding place
I shall conceal myself within the grass
I shall conceal myself in the little plants
I shall conceal myself in the big plants
I will conceal myself in Arali's gullies."
Geshtinanna and the friend of Dumuzi answered, saying,
"O Dumuzi, if we did reveal to anyone your hiding place,
Then may your dogs consume us,
Both your black shepherding dogs,
And your royal pedigreed hounds
Then may your dogs consume us!"

Then the short *galla* said to the tall *galla*,
"You, motherless and fatherless *galla*,
You who are without sister or brother, or wife or children,
You who hover above the Heaven and Earth like watchers,
You who hang close at the man's side,
You who reveal no bias, who cannot discern good from evil,
Tell me, has anyone seen a scared man with a carefree soul?
Ought we then to seek for Dumuzi within his friend's house?
Should we then seek Dumuzi at his brother-in-law's house?

Let us rather seek Dumuzi in his sister Geshtinanna's home."
And the *galla* were pleased with this,
As they went forth to locate Dumuzi
They arrived at Geshtinanna's house, and shouted at her,
"Tell us your brother's whereabouts!"
Geshtinanna refused to answer them
Thus they made offer of the Water Gift to her; she refused it
Thus they made offer of the Grain Gift to her; she refused it
The Heavens were presented, and the Earth was presented,
Still Geshtinanna uttered not a word
Thus they ripped off her garments,
They poured pitch upon her genitals
Still Geshtinanna uttered not a word
Then the short *galla* said to the tall *galla*,
Has there been anyone since time began,
Who ever knew a sister that divulged her brother's hideaway?
Rather, let us proceed to the home of the friend of Dumuzi!"
The *galla* went to the friend of Dumuzi,
And they made offer of the Water Gift to him; he received it
And they made offer of the Grain Gift to him; he received it
So he informed them, "Dumuzi is concealed in the tall grass,
However, I don't know the exact spot."
And thus the *galla* looked for Dumuzi within the tall grass,
But they were not able to uncover him
The friend said, "Dumuzi is concealed in the little plants,

The Descent of Inanna

However, I don't know the exact spot."
Thus the *galla* looked for Dumuzi within the little plants,
But they were not able to uncover him
The friend said, "Dumuzi is concealed in the large plants,
However, I don't know the exact spot."
Thus the *galla* looked for Dumuzi within the large plants,
But they were not able to uncover him
The friend then said, "Dumuzi is concealed in Arali's gullies
Dumuzi lay low within Arali's gullies."
In Arali's gullies the *galla* seized Dumuzi
Dumuzi went ashen and began weeping, and bawled out,
"My sister has brought me salvation,
But my friend has brought me death!
So when the child of my sister is errant upon the highway,
Let that child be safeguarded, and let that child be blessed!
But when the child of my friend is errant upon the highway,
Rather let that child go missing, let that child be damned!"
Then the *galla* demons encircled Dumuzi,
They bound his hands and clamped his neck
Then they battered the husband of Inanna
And Dumuzi lifted up his arms to Heaven,
And to Utu, the god of justice, he implored:
"Utu, my brother-in-law, I married your sister
It was I who brought the meal into the temple
It was I who carried nuptial gifts to Uruk

It was I who kissed upon those blessed lips
It was I who sported on the sacred knees, Inanna's knees!
(O Utu, god of uprightness and of boundless compassion,)
Please alter my hands that they are like those of a gazelle,
And alter my feet that they become like those of a gazelle
Set me free from my demons; allow me to flee to Kubiresh!"
And the compassionate Utu was guided by Dumuzi's plea
Thus he altered his hands to become like those of a gazelle,
So too he altered his feet to become like those of a gazelle
And Dumuzi escaped from his demons, fleeing to Kubiresh
So the *galla* said, "We will go to Kubiresh."
And the *galla* went and came to Kubiresh

Dumuzi escaped from his demons, and fled to Old Belili
So the *galla* said, "We'll go to Old Belili."
And Dumuzi came into Old Belili's house, and said to her,
"Know, ancient woman, that I am not just another mortal,
Rather I am the goddess Inanna's husband
Thus pour out water that I might drink,
And shake some flour that I might eat."
When the aged woman had poured water
And shaken flour for Dumuzi, she went from the house
The *galla* observed her go and then came into the house
But Dumuzi fled away from his demons
And he went to the sheep farm of Geshtinanna, his sister,

The Descent of Inanna

Geshtinanna wept when she saw Dumuzi at her sheep farm
And her mouth went as high as Heaven,
And her mouth went as low as the Earth
Her sorrow spread out to the far horizon like an afghan
She scratched at her eyes, at her mouth, and at her thighs
And the *galla* came over the reed fence
The first *galla* hit Dumuzi on the cheek with a sharp nail
The second *galla* hit Dumuzi's other cheek with a crook
The third *galla* broke the churn's base
The fourth *galla* knocked the drinking cup from its hook
The fifth *galla* broke the churn to bits
The sixth *galla* broke the cup to bits
While the seventh *galla* called to him,
"Dumuzi, the husband of Inanna, the son of Sirtur, arise!
Brother of Geshtinanna, arise from your feigned slumber
Your ewes have been taken; your lambs have been taken
Your goats have been taken; your kids have been taken
Strip from your head the holy crown
Strip from your body the godly robes of the divine Arts
Allow your regal rod to slip to the floor
Strip from your feet the sacred sandals
You will come with us wholly unclothed."
Then the *galla* encircled Dumuzi and grabbed hold of him,
Binding his hands and clamping his neck
Idle sits the churn, unfilled the milk urn,

The cup is broken, Dumuzi is forsaken,
And the sheep farm is lost to the winds!

Then a wailing cry arose within the city,[17]
"My Lady cries in great sorrow for her young husband,
Inanna cries in great sorrow for her youthful husband
Sorrow for the husband, sorrow for her young husband,
Sorrow for her house, sorrow for her city
Dumuzi was captured within Uruk
He will not bathe anymore in Eridu
He will not rinse in the holy shrine
He will no more accept Inanna's mother as his own mother
He will no more engage in dalliances with the city's virgins
He will not rival with the city's youths
He will not bring his sword high above the *kurgarra* priests
Dumuzi's mourners are in great sorrow!"
Inanna too cried tears for her Dumuzi,
"My husband is not, O tender husband,
My love exists no longer, O tender love,
My dearest was snatched from the city
Hear me you flies who hover the prairie,
My dearest lover was ripped from me
So I could not put a shroud about him
The wild buffalo bull is no longer living,
The shepherd, the wild buffalo is gone

The Descent of Inanna

Dumuzi, the wild buffalo, lives no longer
I seek an answer from the hills and valleys, saying to them:
'No longer am I able to serve him food
No longer am I able to bring him beer.'
Now the jackal kips down on his bed
Now the raven nests in the sheep pen
You inquire about his pipe of reeds,
But now the wind must, in his place, blow the sweet notes
You inquire about his pleasing songs,
But now the wind must, in his place, voice the sweet tones."
Dumuzi's mother, Sirtur, likewise wept tears for her son,
"My heart plays sorely upon the mourning pipe of reeds
For my son once walked freely upon the open prairie,
But now he has been taken away
For Dumuzi once walked freely upon the open prairie,
But now he has been bound fast
And the ewe has given up her lamb,
And the goat has given up her kid
My heart plays sorely upon the mourning pipe of reeds
O capricious prairie, where Dumuzi had once declared,
'My mother knows where to find me.'
Now his hands cannot move, now his feet cannot move
My heart plays sorely upon the mourning pipe of reeds
I would now desire to go to him;
I would now wish to see my son!"

His mother trod to the forsaken spot
Sirtur walked the entire way to where Dumuzi was laid out
She gazed at the fallen wild buffalo,
She looked into his face and spoke,
"O my child, it is you, but your spirit is no longer within you
Lamentations fill the house, sorrow fills the private rooms."

Meanwhile, his sister walked the city,
Sobbing for the sake of her brother
Geshtinanna walked aimlessly the city,
Sobbing for the memory of Dumuzi,
"O Dumuzi, why did the *galla* take you
O brother, why did the *galla* take you
No longer will I see the shepherd tending the sheep farm
No longer will I see my brother, Dumuzi, walk the prairie
Brother, I would freely take your place
I would go to the Underworld myself,
And release you from your cruel fate."
Geshtinanna went to Inanna and said,
"No longer will I see the shepherd tending the sheep farm
No longer will I see my brother, Dumuzi, walk the prairie
I would freely take my brother's place
I would go to the Underworld myself,
And release him from his cruel fate."
And Inanna replied to Geshtinanna,

The Descent of Inanna

"Come, let us seek Dumuzi together."
And they walked and looked for the shepherd Dumuzi,
They travelled and searched for Geshtinanna's brother
All over the sheep farm did they look,
All across the prairies did they search,
But Dumuzi could not be found anywhere they looked
And when Geshtinanna was despairing for her brother,
At that moment a fly came near them
The blessed fly circled overhead above Inanna and spoke,
"If I let you know where Dumuzi is,
What will you offer me in return?"
And Inanna replied, "If you tell me,
Then I will allow you to enter into the beer halls and taverns,
I will let you hang about the discourses of the learned men,
I will allow you to flitter about the singing of the songsters."
And thus the fly spoke in reply to them,
"Then raise your eyes to the prairie's border, gaze unto Arali,
There will you find Geshtinanna's brother
There will you find Dumuzi, the shepherd."*
Thus Inanna and Geshtinanna went to the prairie's border,
And Dumuzi was there crying tears of woe
Inanna then took Dumuzi's hand and said,
"You will enter into the Underworld for half of the year,

---

* Arali, also known as Arallu, was a mythical desert region at the edge of the world, and on the borderland of the underworld (and which also appears in the Canaanite myth 'Baal').

And your sister, who has agreed, will enter the other half
On the day that you are summoned, you will be captured
On the day Geshtinanna is summoned, you shall be freed!"
Thus did Inanna leave Dumuzi in the grip of eternal fate!

O holy Ereshkigal, your glory is great!
O holy Ereshkigal, I sing your praises!

THE EPIC OF ANZU

TABLET 1

I raise my song for the glorious son of the world's sovereign,

Cherished of Mami, and offspring of the mighty god, Ellil!

I sing the praises of glorious Nimrod, the beloved of Mami,[*]

And the son of the mighty god, Ellil; the offspring of Ekur,[†]

Who rules the Anunnaki, is revered in the temple of Eninnu,[‡]

Who supplies water to cattle stalls, and for garden channels,

And for reservoirs, both within the city and in the countryside

He is truly a warrior, whose attack is akin to the flood-surge

It is he who leaves the war sash crimson-stained with blood

Thus do even the most savage and merciless of *gallu*-demons,

Shudder with trepidation whenever he raises his battle-cry!

Hear the praises of the might of this superlative man of steel,

Who when frenzied conquered and bound Stone Mountain,

Whose weapon also came to defeat the high-flying Anzu bird,

And who killed the bull-man who dwelt within the great sea[§]

A war man of mettle, dealing swift death with his battle-arms

Fearless one, who readily assembles into ranks his war legions

---

[*] Nimrod is the familiar version of the name from the Bible, but in Mesopotamia it was Ninurta. Mami, his mother, is the mother goddess of Mesopotamia.
[†] Ellil is the god of the atmosphere, while Ekur is Ellil's temple but is also used as a name for the god himself.
[‡] Eninnu is temple to Ningirsu ('Girsu's Lord'), a god of fertility and war.
[§] Apart from his contest with the Anzu bird contained herein, nothing further is known of his other two exploits.

The Epic of Anzu

At this time, however, there was yet no stage made for the Igigi,

And the Igigi were wont to gather to receive their Ellil-power[*]

The great rivers, the Tigris and Euphrates, had come into being

Yet this was before the founts had given water unto the land,

Before the seas **filled their basins to the very edge of the world**

The clouds were yet distant, upon the far horizon **roundabout**

All the Igigi came together to the gods' warrior, their father Ellil

His sons, the Igigi, brought news, and raising their voices said,

"Take heed, for the words which we will speak are entirely true

In distant regions, upon a forested mountain known as Hehe,

There within the very heart of the Anunnaki's **far-flung realm**

These same outlying lands have given birth to the Anzu bird

Know that its beak is alike to a saw **with countless serrations,**

And by all accounts his talons are like piercing hooks of iron,

Which **could tear to shreds the very firmament of the heavens!**

There are eleven breastplates **which are layered upon his chest**

The mountains have become his nest, **and their peaks his perch**

And this being the very sierra which harbors the four winds,

That when he makes his shriek **thus he stirs up the west wind,**

And the south wind **too, which comes to parch the countryside**

The strong **east** wind he **likewise brings, which fells tall cedars,**

And too the masses **of frost which blow down from the north**

Whirlwinds **which stir mightily, wreaking havoc on the plains,**

They all came together as **he gathered them beneath his wings**

---

[*] The Igigi are lesser gods of the heavens and ruled by Ellil

Tablet I

Thus not only the four winds **but the whirlwinds too are his."**
Then Ellil, the gods' father, the god of Duranki, studied him,[*]
And yet he betrayed not a single indication of his impressions,
But rather he examined Anzu up close **with inquisitive eyes,**
Deliberating the matter with himself **in great consternation,**
"Who is the one that laid **the egg giving rise to this creature?**
Why has this **terrifying foul been brought here before me?"**
Ea rose to provide answer to the questions his heart sought,
And the wise, far-seeing one spoke his words to Ellil, saying,
"It must have arisen from the waters of the Great Flood itself
It could only have been the sacred founts of the Apsu's gods
And thus it must have been conceived within the wide Earth,
And he emerged into this world from the rock-strewn sierra
But as you've seen Anzu **now,** have him serve you for all time!
Let him guard the way to your central chamber, henceforth!
Let him be there too when you bathe in the purified waters,
And also, let him watch over the objects of your Ellil-power."
Ellil heard and considered everything that was spoken to him,
Then he selected the place for a cult center **in the city Nippur**
He had the power to give commands to every one of the gods
And produced a new destiny that Anzu might take charge of
Ellil made him guard over the entryway of his sacred chamber
He was there too when he bathed himself in the purified water,

---

[*] Duranki is Ellil's temple, meaning 'linking earth and heaven', as Ellil is a god of the intermediate region (that is, the atmosphere).

The Epic of Anzu

Within clear view before him were the objects of his Ellil-power:
Majestic crown, fine robe, and Tablet of Fate within his hands
Anzu looked at these and at Duranki's god, father of the gods,
And he made up his mind to take the Ellil-power for himself
Anzu time and again looked at Duranki's god, the gods' father,
And he was determined to acquire the Ellil-power for himself,
"The Tablet of Fate will no longer be the gods' but will be mine!
I will have the power to give commands to every one of the gods,
I will have the throne for myself and dictate all manner of rites,
And also, I will be the commander-in-chief of all of the Igigi!"
Such did he contemplate rebellious intentions within his heart,
And there in the hall, at the entrance to Ellil's private rooms,
From the place where he usually looked, anticipated morning
So while Ellil undertook his ablutions in the purified water,
Entirely naked, having left his crown sitting upon his throne,
Thus it was that he took the Tablet of Fate, the Ellil-power,
All rites were neglected once Anzu took wing and vanished
With not a glimmer of light, and not a whisper to be heard

The advisor of the gods, their father Ellil, was at a total loss,
Because the gleam had been stolen from his private rooms
(And every one of the Igigi was overcome with bewilderment,)*
(Because the gleam had been stolen from his private rooms)

---

*These two lines, and other inserted parenthetical lines, are added from the OBV (Old Babylonian version).

Tablet I

So the gods from all places sought everywhere for an answer

Anu raised his voice, speaking to his sons, the gods, saying,

"The god who kills Anzu will acquire fame across the globe!"[*]

Thus they summoned Anu's son Adad, manager of canals[†]

And the Overlord raised his voice to be heard, saying to him,

"Great and fearsome Adad, whose charge cannot be stemmed,

Go and sear Anzu with your powerful weapon, the lightning!

And your name will gain fame within the congress of the gods

None of your brothers, the gods, could claim to be your equal,

And surely you will find that temples will be erected for you!

Your cult centers will emerge everywhere in the four quarters,

And so too your cult centers shall be established within Ekur!

Reveal your might before the gods, and you will be supreme!"

And Adad gave his reply, speaking to his father Anu, saying,

"Father, would anyone eagerly go to that remote mountain?

Which of your sons, the gods, do you think could beat Anzu?

He holds the Tablet of Fate, and possession of the Ellil-power;

All rites were neglected once Anzu took wing and vanished

No longer does Duranki's god dictate all commands, he does!

Just in pronouncing the words any he curses will turn to clay

Thus the gods must dread whatever invocation he might utter!"

And, turning about, declared he would make no such journey

---

[*] This is modified slightly using the OBV. Anu is the supreme god of the heavens, and here the Overlord.
[†] Adad is more importantly the storm god

Thus they summoned next to them Gerra, the son of Anunitu

And the Overlord raised his voice to be heard, saying to him,

"Great and fearsome Gerra, whose charge cannot be stemmed,

Go and strike Anzu with your powerful weapon, the wildfire!

And your name will gain fame within the congress of the gods

None of your brothers, the gods, could claim to be your equal,

And surely you will find that temples will be erected for you!

Your cult centers will emerge everywhere in the four quarters,

And so too your cult centers shall be established within Ekur!

Reveal your might before the gods, and you will be supreme!"

And Gerra gave his reply, speaking to his father Anu, saying,

"Father, would anyone eagerly go to that remote mountain?

Which of your sons, the gods, do you think could beat Anzu?

He holds the Tablet of Fate, and possession of the Ellil-power;

All rites were neglected once Anzu took wing and vanished

No longer does Duranki's god dictate all commands, he does!

Just in pronouncing the words any he curses will turn to clay

Thus the gods must dread whatever invocation he might utter!"

And, turning about, declared he would make no such journey

Thus they summoned next to them Shara, the son of Ishtar

And the Overlord raised his voice, making a proposal, saying,

"Great and fearsome Shara, whose charge cannot be stemmed,

Go and hit Anzu with your powerful weapon, **the earthquake!**

And your name will gain fame within the congress of the gods

Tablet I

None of your brothers, the gods, could claim to be your equal,
And surely you will find that temples will be erected for you!
Your cult centers will emerge everywhere in the four quarters,
And so too your cult centers shall be established within Ekur!
Reveal your might before the gods, and you will be supreme!"
And Shara gave his reply, speaking to his father Anu, saying,
"Father, would anyone eagerly go to that remote mountain?
Which of your sons, the gods, do you think could beat Anzu?
He holds the Tablet of Fate, and possession of the Ellil-power;
All rites were neglected once Anzu took wing and vanished
No longer does Duranki's god dictate all commands, he does!
Just in pronouncing the words any he curses will turn to clay
Thus the gods must dread whatever invocation he might utter!"
And, turning about, declared he would make no such journey

In such a hopeless situation the gods were at a loss for words
At their seats even the Igigi were despairing, deeply depressed
Then the master of thought, from the Apsu, and full of wisdom,
Ea formed an idea within himself; his heart devised a solution,
He conveyed to Anu what he had considered in deep thought,
"Bestow unto me authority that I might go and make a search,
And select from amongst the congress to identify Anzu's slayer
I will go forth and conduct this search among the gods myself,
And select from amongst the congress to identify Anzu's slayer."
Hearing his words the Igigi, no longer troubled, kissed his feet

The Epic of Anzu

Then the far-seeing one, holy Ea, raised his voice to be heard,
And spoke, intending his words be heard by Anu and Dagan,
"Send word to Belet-ili, the gods' sister, that I seek her presence
She who acts as the judicious adviser to her brothers, the gods
Assure that her supreme status is declared within the congress,
And the gods bestow unto her high honors within the congress
I will then disclose to her the plan I have devised in my heart."
And they gave word that the gods' sister, Belet-ili, was sought;
She who acts as the judicious adviser to her brothers, the gods;
Assured that her supreme status was declared in the congress,
And the gods bestowed unto her high honors in the congress
Then Ea disclosed to her the plan he had devised in his heart,
"Before now we have referred to you by the name of Mami,
But henceforth you shall be called 'Mistress of all the Gods'!
Propose this to the strong man, your most famous dear one,
With great power, who calls the ranks of legions for battle!
Go and propose this to Nimrod, your most famed dear one,
(With great power, who calls together the battle-ready Seven!)
And he shall be addressed as 'Lord' within the gods' congress
Revealing his might to the gods, his name will be supreme!
That his name will be extolled throughout the entire world
And so too his cult center **shall be established within Ekur,**
And 'Lord **of the High Gods' will be the title he will bear!"**
All who heard were glad at the wise counselor's utterance,
While the Igigi remained silent, filled with apprehension

Tablet I

(And Mami heard every word which he had spoken to her,)

(Then the peerless one, Belet-ili, answered him, "Certainly!")

(And the gods of the earth received her reply with great joy,)

(And the Igigi were no longer troubled, and kissed her feet)

(Then she asked her son to join her within the gods' congress,)

(And she gave counsel to her beloved, before Anu and Dagan,)

Declaring the purpose of their actions before the congress,

"I gave birth to all of the Igigi, and I also made the Anunnaki,

So too I brought this very congress of the gods into existence,

And it was I who conferred upon my brother his Ellil-power,

I also judged that the rule of the heavens would go to Anu,

But this Anzu has disrupted the cosmic order I had set forth

He has gained the Tablet of Fate, which I myself designated,

Is guilty of stealing from Ellil; he has overthrown your father,

And has usurped all the rites, using them for his own sake!"

(So choose the right direction, and set the designated hour)

TABLET II

So choose the right direction, and set the designated hour,

And may the morning glow shine for those I made, the gods

Gather together from every corner your merciless war force

And as they conquer him, cause your hostile winds to blast,

Conquer high-flying Anzu, bring peace to the lands I made,[*]

Obliterate his lair, and let dread resound around his head

Have the fear of your war army unsettle him to his very core[†]

Cause the destructive whirlwind to rear up to spar with him

Place your arrow, once dipped in poison, on the bow-string

Make your visage alter, like the shape-shifting *gallu*-demon

(May he become terror-filled from the curses you yell at him)

(Let him be lost in the dark, his eyes become feeble and blind,)

(And let him not escape, but may his wings be lost in battle!)

Cast forth a mist, that he might not perceive your appearance

Unleash your beams above him, and your offensive lofty leap,

With a sear greater than even Shamash is capable of making

(Let the moon darken, and the day's light be like night to him)[‡]

Grasp his neck within your hand, and bring doom to Anzu

May the wind then scatter his feathers to declare good tidings,

---

[*] Modified using the OBV, the original reads: "Capture high-flying Anzu; spread over all the lands I made"

[†] Two missing lines here in the OBV but likewise not present in the Standard Babylonian version, perhaps indicate these OBV tablets were copied after damage was done to these lines.

[‡] OBV line, the original reads: "And may the extensive light of day become darkness to him"

Tablet II

That they might come to Ekur, the home of your father Ellil
Spread over the entire sierra, and cut the throat of evil Anzu
Then will the right to kingly rule lie within Ekur once more,
Then will the rites once again be with your progenitor father,
And surely you will find that temples will be erected for you!
Your cult centers will emerge everywhere in the four quarters,
And so too your cult centers shall be established within Ekur!
Reveal your might before the gods, and you will be supreme!"
The warrior heard every word that his mother spoke to him,
Feeling able and supremely strong, he went to a hidden place,
And in secrecy the Lord called together the battle-ready Seven[*]
There the warrior assembled together the seven hostile winds,
These being the seven cyclones, who stir up dust at their feet
Thereby he gathered together from every quarter a war army[†]
And he went to engage in battle with a frightening entourage
Even the tempests travelled calmly with him, ready to strike!

On the side of the mountain Anzu and Nimrod met together
Anzu gazed upon him, and bristled with wrath against him,
Thrusting forward, and flashing his teeth like an *umu*-demon
His Mantle of Brilliance cast its glow over the entire mountain
Expelling a roar like a riled lion, and seething with distemper,
He raised his voice to be heard, bellowing at him, and saying,

---

[*] These last two lines are influenced by the OBV.
[†] In the OBV the summoning of the seven winds is performed by the Great Goddess, Mami.

65

The Epic of Anzu

"Yes, I am the one who seized for myself every one of the rites,
Holding the power to give commands to every one of the gods
Give your name, and declare why you seek to battle with me!"
Such was the defiant statement which rushed forth at him
The warrior Nimrod gave his reply to Anzu, speaking thus:
"I come as **avenger** of Duranki's god, who founded Duranki,
The **navel** of the wide earth occupied by Ea, the Lord of Fate,
Coming to **this sierra** to declare war, to crush you underfoot!
(**Nothing will save you: not the winds,** whirlwinds, or armor!")[*]
Hearing him Anzu gave an irate screech among the mounts,
Dark fell upon the mountain, its sides blackened by shadow,
And the god's candle, Shamash, was obscured by darkness
Adad expelled a roar like a lion, adding to the din of Anzu
Impending war brewed between the two battle formations
The Flood-weapon gathered, the armored chest became red,
Showered with death, flashing arrows bolted like lightning
The two armies stirred up all the resounding roar of warfare
And then that superb strong man, the glorious son of Mami,
Held in trust by Anu and Dagan, loved by the far-seeing god,
Placed an arrow upon his bow-string, pulling it back fully;
Directing the arrow in his direction, shot from the bent bow
Yet it did not come anywhere near Anzu, but was deflected
Anzu raised his voice to be heard, and screeching at it, said,

---

[*] This line, likewise in the OBV but not the Standard Babylonian version, might have been left out due to early damage of the tablet.

66

"Arrow-shaft that was on its way, go back to your reed bed!
And bow, get yourself back to your grove! And bow-string,
Go back into the ram's innards; feathers, back to your birds!"
He had possession of the gods' Tablet of Fate within his hand
It swayed the bow-string, so the arrows came nowhere near
A stunned calm spread over the combat zone, the war halted,
Their arms set aside, unable to take Anzu among the mounts
Then Nimrod called out and gave orders to Sharur, saying,
"Report to Ea, the far-seeing, what unfolds before your eyes!
Convey this word of the Lord: Nimrod was surrounding Anzu,
Warrior Nimrod, enveloped in the dust-cloud of destruction,
Placed an arrow upon his bow-string, pulling it back fully;
Directing the arrow in his direction, shot from the bent bow
Yet it did not come anywhere near Anzu, but was deflected
Anzu raised his voice to be heard, and screeching at it, said,
'Arrow-shaft that was on its way, go back to your reed bed!
And bow, get yourself back to your grove! And bow-string,
Go back to the ram's innards; feathers, back to your birds!'
He had possession of the gods' Tablet of Fate within his hand
It swayed the bow-string, so the arrows came nowhere near
A stunned calm spread over the combat zone, the war halted,
Their arms set aside, unable to take Anzu among the mounts."
So Sharur bent low and carried the communication dispatch,
And he conveyed the war message to the far-seeing god, to Ea
All that the Lord had spoken to him, thus did he repeat to Ea:

The Epic of Anzu

"This is the word of the Lord: Nimrod was surrounding Anzu,
Warrior Nimrod, enveloped in the dust-cloud of destruction,
Placed an arrow upon his bow-string, pulling it back fully;
Directing the arrow in his direction, shot from the bent bow
Yet it did not come anywhere near Anzu, but was deflected,
Anzu raised his voice to be heard, and screeching at it, said,
'Arrow-shaft that was on its way, go back to your reed bed!
And bow, get yourself back to your grove! And bow-string,
Go back to the ram's innards; feathers, back to your birds!'
He had possession of the gods' Tablet of Fate within his hand
It swayed the bow-string, so the arrows came nowhere near
A stunned calm spread over the combat zone, the war halted
Their arms set aside, unable to take Anzu among the mounts."
And the far-seeing god heard every word his son sent to him
And then he raised his voice, and gave these orders to Sharur,
"Now you must, in turn, convey these words back to your lord,
And reiterate to him every word I am about to relate to you:
Do not abandon your diligence, but rather go on to triumph!
You must wear him down as the tempests clash, so he molts
Then after you have released your arrows, use your battle axe
To slash off his wings; take off both the right and the left one
But at the sight of his wings before his eyes, uttering this cry,
'My wing, my wing', do not at that point lose your courage
Pull tight your bow's arc, that arrows fly like lightning bolts
Make his wing feathers flit in the air amongst the entire host

68

Tablet II

Then finally, grasp him about his neck so as to defeat Anzu
May the wind then scatter his feathers to declare good tidings,
That they might come to Ekur, the home of your father Ellil
Spread over the entire sierra, and cut the throat of evil Anzu
Then will the right to kingly rule lie within Ekur once more,
Then will the rites once again be with your progenitor father,
And surely you will find that temples will be erected for you!
Your cult centers will emerge everywhere in the four quarters!
And so too your cult centers shall be established within Ekur!
Reveal your might before the gods, and you will be supreme!"
So Sharur bent low and carried the communication dispatch
And he, in turn, conveyed this war message back to his lord
All that Ea had spoken to him, thus did he reiterate to him:
"Do not abandon your diligence, but rather go on to triumph!
You must wear him down as the tempests clash, and he molts
Then after you have released your arrows, use your battle axe
To slash off his wings; take off both the right and the left one
But at the sight of his wings before his eyes, uttering this cry,
'My wing, my wing', do not at that point lose your courage,
Pull tight your bow's arc, that arrows fly like lightning bolts
Make his wing feathers flit in the air amongst the entire host
Then finally, grasp him about the neck so as to defeat Anzu
May the wind then scatter his feathers to declare good tidings,
That they might come to Ekur, the home of your father Ellil,
Spread over the entire sierra, and cut the throat of evil Anzu

Then will the right to kingly rule lie within Ekur once more,
Then will the rites once again be with your progenitor father,
And surely you will find that temples will be erected for you!
Your cult centers will emerge everywhere in the four quarters!
And so too your cult centers shall be established within Ekur!
Reveal your might before the gods, and you will be supreme!"
And the warrior heard every word sent by Ea, the far-seeing
Feeling able and supremely strong, he went to a hidden place
And in secrecy the Lord called together the battle-ready Seven:
There the warrior assembled together the seven hostile winds,
These being the seven cyclones, who stir up dust at their feet
And thus gathered together from every quarter a war army
And he went to engage in war with a frightening entourage
Even the tempests travelled calmly with him, ready to strike!
(On the side of the mountain Anzu and Nimrod met together)

TABLET III

On the side of the mountain Anzu and Nimrod met together
The foundation of the world shook, earthquakes abounded,
Dark fell upon his mountain, the heavenly sky turned gray
Destruction **and death was raining down all over the earth,**
Blazing heat seared, disorder **spread wide across the world**
A storm **current of violence was sweeping** to the four winds
Their weapons had driven away any aid from the cool air,
As both of them were now wet with sweat from their warfare,
And Anzu was worn down in the tempests clash, and molted
So Nimrod, after releasing his arrows, took up his battle axe,
And with it slashed off his wings; both the right and the left
And when Anzu spied both of his wings and uttered his cry
Yet as he shrieked "My wing, my wing" an arrow struck him,
A missile pierced him through to the chambers of his heart
Nimrod caused his shaft to penetrate his pinion and wing;
A missile pierced him through both his heart and his lungs
Thus he conquered the mountains, overcame their lowlands;
Nimrod conquered the mountains, overcame their lowlands
In his battle frenzy he spread his army over the entire land,
He spread into the heart of the sierra, and killed vile Anzu
Warrior Nimrod retook the gods' Tablet of Fate in his hand
The breeze scattered Anzu's feathers, declaring good tidings
And Dagan witnessed this gospel and was heartily pleased

71

Summoning every one of the gods, with great cheer he said,

"It is so that the strong man has killed Anzu on his mount,

And holds in his hands again the **power**s of Anu and Dagan

So let him come that he might celebrate, be joyful and festive

To stand among his brothers, the gods; to learn their secrets

That he might become fully aware of the mysteries of the gods

And that Ellil, the **wise counselor** of his brothers, the gods,

Might likewise confer unto him every one of the sacred rites."

Ellil raised his voice to be heard, speaking to Dagan, saying,

"**Like the flood**-water **Nimrod has inundated the mountains**

In his **battle frenzy he spread his army** over the entire land

And when within the heart of the sierra he killed vile Anzu

Warrior Nimrod retook the gods' Tablet of Fate in his hand

So invite him back home, that he might make his way here,

That he might restore the Tablet of Fate into your possession."

So Ellil raised his voice, speaking to his officer Nusku, saying,

"Go forth from here, Nusku, and escort Birdu here before me."

And thus Nusku went forth and brought Birdu before Ellil

Ellil raised his voice to be heard, speaking to Birdu, saying,

"Birdu, I will send you forth; I will **send you before Nimrod,**

To convey the words which have been sent by his father Ellil:

'The gods know you killed vile Anzu in the heart of the sierra

Being heartily pleased and cheered they then summoned me,

And I was ordered to come before you and speak Ellil's words

So please go to him now, that he might give you due praise!'"

And thus Birdu went forth and made his way before Nimrod

Nimrod raised his voice to be heard, speaking to Birdu, saying,

"Birdu, for what reason do you come to me with such urgency?"

Birdu raised his voice to be heard, speaking to Nimrod, saying,

"Lord, your father Ellil sent me **forth** to convey these words:

'The gods know you killed vile Anzu in the heart of the sierra

Being heartily pleased and cheered **they then summoned me,**

And I was ordered to come before you and **speak Ellil's words**

So please go to him now, that he might **give you due praise!**'"[18]

※

And Birdu raised his voice to be heard, saying to Nimrod,

"...Go with the corpse of your conquered foe to Ellil's temple,

That there he might, in all of his glory, look upon evil Anzu

And you, warrior, mighty as when you conquered the mount,[*]

And likewise destroyed high-flying Anzu in all his strength

Since you possessed such courage and defeated the mountain,

So all enemies prostrated themselves before your father, Ellil

Since you, Nimrod, with such courage defeated the mountain,

So all enemies prostrated themselves before your father, Ellil

You have gained total command, and also every rite is yours

Is there any being in existence who is comparable with you?

---

[*] A reference to his previously mentioned exploit referred to in Tablet 1, the otherwise unknown defeat of Stone Mountain.

The highest honors are given, the Fate gods' temples yours
And Nissaba* will arrive to perform the holy rites for you

In the furrowed farmland they refer to you as NINGIRSU,
And they crown you the shepherd of the entire population
And they utilize your honored name of DUKU as regal title
You are called HURABTIL in Elam, SHUSHINAK in Susa
With the title LORD OF THE MYSTERIES in Anu's heaven
When among your brothers, the gods, you are called Ellil
And thus you are called by the same name as your father,
....who marches at the vanguard
In Egalmah you are PABILSAG, in Ur you are.......................
And in Ekumah they refer to you by the name of NINAZU
....for Duranki was where you were born
In..........................they refer of you by the name of ISHTARAN
In...you are known as ZABABA
....is how they refer to you
Among all of the gods your courage is beyond comparison,
And the coronet upon your godhead outshines all of the rest
Thus I might declare without a single reserve that I exalt you!
In..........................they call you by the name of LUGALBANDA
In E-igi-kalama you are referred to as LUGAL-MARADA
And they refer to you in E-sikil as the WARRIOR TISHPAK
In E-nimma-anku they refer to you as.................OF...................

---

* Nissaba is a Sumerian goddess of fertility and writing.

In Kullab they know you by the name URUK'S WARRIOR,
Revered there as the glorious son of your mother Belet-ili
In.............................you are called LORD OF THE LANDMARK
....you are known as PANIGARA
In E-akkil you are called PAPSUKKAL, who leads the march
Your names outshine the other gods by leaps and bounds
Among the gods you are fit and able, cunning and masterful
And your wise counselor, your father Anu, the far-seeing one,
Who oversees all war and conflict, gave you martial insight,
And named you as the general of all of their armed forces"[19]

※

ERRA AND ISHUM

TABLET 1

I raise my song for the son of the world's king and creator
Of Ellil's heir, Hendursanga, who possesses the soaring staff,[*]
Who acts as guide to all peoples, and shepherd of the masses
Of Ishum, the righteous slayer, whose practiced hands wield
His menacing weapons, and make his terrifying axes gleam!
It was when the gods' warlord, Erra, was pacing up and down,
Motivated to engage in warfare, he said to his war weapons,
"Cover your faces with lethal poison!" To the seven Sebitti,
The matchless war-gods, he said, "Take up your armaments!"
Then to Ishum he said, "Into the wide countryside will I go
As your illumination can be seen, be the light that guides,
As the gods march behind you, for you are **the fatal** sword."

So stand up, Erra, and when you conquer the countryside,
How ecstatic you will be, how much your heart will rejoice!
Yet Erra was filled with lethargy as that from lack of sleep,
Saying to himself, "Should I stand or instead go off to bed?"
And then to his weapons, "Stay there, leaning in the closet!"
To the seven Sebitti, matchless war-gods, he raised his voice,
And spoke to them, "And all of you, return to your dwelling."
He will remain at peace in bed, sporting with his wife Mami

---

[*] Hendursanga is another name for Ishum

That is, until such time as you, Ishum, would go to wake him;
For he is called Engidudu, which means 'night-stalking lord'
An example to royalty, bringing life's light to dead of night,
Who gives guidance to youths and maids, bringing serenity
Far different from this are the Sebitti, the matchless war-gods,
For at their unnatural birth were seen countless dire omens
Exhaling deadly breath, anyone seeing them is seized with fear
Standing frozen in place, people are not able to go any nearer
Thus Ishum acts as the gate standing locked in front of them
Know that when the king of the gods, Anu, seeded the Earth
That she bore him these Seven Gods who he called the Sebitti
And when they took their place before him, Anu set their fates
He called forward the first of them, and made this declaration,
"Any place you amass and march forth, none will match you."
To the second he said, "Kindle like Gerra and scorch like fire!"
Then to the third he said, "You will take on the aspect of a lion,
So that any who see you as such would crouch down in fear!"
Then to the fourth he said, "May even the mountain take flight
When faced by the one who wields your savage weaponry!"
Then to the fifth, "Be a gust of wind, and find the sky's edge!"
Then to the sixth, "Trespass high and low, and show no mercy!"
Then the seventh he imbued with a serpent's deadly poison,
And he said to him, "You will bring down all living creatures!"
Then after Anu had designated the fates of each of the Sebitti,
He put them under the command of Erra, the gods' warlord,

Tablet I

And then spoke, saying, "May they stride side-by-side with you!

So when the uproar of civilization is more than you can stand,

And you feel in the mood to unleash your destructive fury,

To strike down some of the people or some of Shakkan's cattle,[*]

They will be your severe weapons, striding abreast with you!"

Certainly they were fearsome; weapons raised, saying to Erra,

"Stand, raise yourself up! For what reason do you remain here,

Residing within the city limits like an elderly man in his dotage?

Why remain safe within your house like the babbling infant?

Is our food to be women's bread, as one who's not gone to war?

Are we to be cowardly and anxious as one with no war scars?

To march onto the battlefield gladdens like the youths' festival!

And anyone who remains within the city, even if he is royalty,

Certainly will not be able to satisfy his hunger on bread alone,

He will be maligned and dishonored from his own people's lips

Likewise, he can no longer criticize those who have gone to war

No matter the physical might of him who remains in the city,

Will he be able to overcome him who has engaged in warfare?

No matter how dainty it might be, the food that is in the city

Has no comparison to that which is smoked over the open fire,

The most full beer, brewed best, nothing like water from a skin,

And the most well-founded edifice, no match for the pup tent

O Warlord Erra, make your way forth onto the field of battle!

O Warlord Erra, go so that your weaponry will mightily ring!

---

[*] Shakkan is the cattle god

Erra and Ishum

Such a great din that those on Heaven and Earth will shudder

Make it so that the Igigi will hear, and thus praise your name

Make it so the Anunnaki will hear your utterances with fear

Make it so the gods will hear, under the power of your yoke

Make it so kings will hear, and bow down to you in obeisance

Make it so countries will hear, and bear their tribute to you

Make it so the demons will hear, that they may not pester you

Make it so the mighty will hear, biting their lips in trepidation

Make it so the highest peaks will hear, and thus crouch in fear

Make it so that the wave-clustered oceans will likewise hear,

Such that they become turbulent and obliterate their bounty

Make it so the tree trunks in the majestic forests lie broken

Make it so the reeds in their thick thickets are mowed flat

Make it so the people are fearful and stunned into silence

Make it so that the cattle will shake, and will become as clay

Make it so your fathers, the gods, notice and extol your valor!

O Warlord Erra, why have you not sought the field of battle,

But remain in the city limits? So that even Shakkan's cattle

And all the other wild animals reveal only contempt for us

O Warlord Erra, while true the things we say may be severe,

Nonetheless, it is something which must be openly revealed,

Given that the entire world is more than we are able to bear

Thus you will be forced to pay attention to all we have said!

And act for the sake of the Anunnaki, who appreciate quiet!

The uproar of the people keeps the Anunnaki from sleeping,

Tablet I

While cattle trod the pastures, lifeblood of the land, to ruin
And the farmer cries tears of woe over his field's pitiful yields
The cattle of Shakkan are brought down by the lion and wolf
While the shepherd beseeches you for the sake of his sheep
For he too is not able to catch a wink of sleep by night or day
And we who took the mountain pass no longer know the way!
The spiders have spun webs upon our accoutrements of war,
Our once reliable bows become stiff, unyielding to our pulls,
Our once wounding arrowheads now dulled into uselessness,
The daggers once wielded tarnished from lack of proper use."
The warlord Erra heard every word which they spoke to him
And the Sebitti's speech was as pleasing to him as purified oil
And thus he raised his voice to be heard, speaking to Ishum,
"Can you just stand there and not utter even a single word?
Rather make way that I might set forth upon the highway!
I will enlist the matchless warrior-gods, the Sebitti, **to fight**
And they will stride side-by-side with me, my fearsome arms
While you may either march at the vanguard or at the rear."
And after Ishum had listened to his words, he was concerned
He raised his voice to be heard, speaking to the warlord Erra,
"But Lord Erra, for what reason do you turn upon the gods?
And given that you've made plans to conquer entire nations,
Wiping out their citizens, can I appeal to you to stand down?"
Erra raised his voice to be heard, and spoke his words plainly,
Speaking his words to Ishum, who marches at his vanguard,

Erra and Ishum

"Refrain from speaking, Ishum, and hear what I have to say,

Concerning the citizens that you suggest I ought to spare

O wise Ishum, at the gods' vanguard, you give wise counsel

I am a buffalo bull in Heaven; I am the lion upon the Earth,

Of all lands I am emperor, and am severe amongst the gods

And you must know that I am a man of war among the Igigi

Likewise that I am a redoubtable force among the Anunnaki,

I am a predator among cattle, a feral ram among the mounts,

I am Gerra in reed-beds, the chopping-axe in the woodlands,

And I am the banner spanning over entire campaigns of war,

I gust as the wind does, and thunder like Adad is given to do,

Like Shamash I can behold the very distant cusp of the world

And when I am upon the field of battle, I am like a feral sheep,

I move out into the pastureland, and this becomes my home

While every other of the gods lacks the courage to make war

And this is precisely why the entire people think less of them

Thus, because they no longer tremble in fright at my name,

And self-serving King Marduk has not lived up to his word,[*]

Thus will I go out and stir up the wrath within King Marduk

Thus will I call him from his abode, and overcome his people

Thus did the warlord Erra go out in the direction of Shuanna[†]

Thus did he go all the way to the city of the king of the gods

And he went into Esagila, the temple of Heaven and Earth[*]

---

[*] Marduk is the foremost king of the Babylonian gods, who features prominently in their creation epic 'Enuma Elish'

[†] Shuanna is another name for Babylon

Tablet I

And took his place before Marduk, saying to the gods' king,

"For what reason do your robes, which decorate his lordship,

Which once sparkled as the heavenly stars, become smirched?

And his lordship's crown, which once lit the hall of E-halanki,

Causing it to glow like E-temen-anki, has now been dulled!"[†]

Thus the gods' king raised his voice to Erra, the gods' warrior,

"O Warlord Erra, of relevance to what you declare you'll do,

There was a time, quite a while ago, when I became enraged

And went from my house to make preparations for a Flood

I went from my house, disordering both Heaven and Earth

Even the heights of the sky shook, the heaven's stars shifted

And I never even restored them back to where they had been

Erkalla was struck by earthquake,[‡] the plowed field's yield fell

So from then 'til now it's been difficult to gain a fruitful crop

Yea, as I say, even the order of the Heaven and Earth was lost

Until the founts ebbed and the waters of the flood withdrew

So I went back and gazed all around; the result was horrific

There were very few survivors amongst all the progeny of life

And I never sought to replenish them to what they had been

Such that I was like the plowman, holding seed in his hand

Thus I made for myself a dwelling which would be my home

Yet regarding my robes, being soiled and spoiled by the Flood,

Gerra brought brightness back to me, and purified my robes

---

[*] Esagila is Marduk's temple
[†] E-halanki is the temple of Zarpanitum and E-temen-anki is Marduk's ziggurat in Babylon.
[‡] Erkalla is the underworld

And once he had caused them to shine, completing his task,
I set the royal crown on my head, and returned to my palace
Then was my form restored to full glory, my stare formidable!
But then regarding the humans who had survived the Flood,
And who had witnessed the consequences of what I had done,
Is it right that I lift my weapons to extinguish this vestige too?
It was I who sent the Artisans, the Seven Sages, into the Apsu
And it was I too who told them that they were not to return,
And I who altered where the *mesu*-tree and *elmesu*-stone were,
Telling no one; but then, returning to what you declared to do
Where could the *mesu*-tree, whose wood is the gods' being, be?
Further, it is a fitting emblem of the world's Supreme Power
That unspoiled beam, lofty virgin, from whom gods are made
The roots of which stretch all the way down into the deep sea
Beneath a hundred leagues of water, to the bottom of Arallu[*]
And with its crown stretching above to touch Anu's heaven
Did you find the flawless *ziginduru*-stone **the Artisans** lost?
Where could Nin-ildu be, the craftsman of my Anu-power?
Wielding the sun's unsullied axe, knowing the timbers' **traits**,
The one that makes the night glow like the day in brilliance,
And thus causes the people to prostrate themselves at my feet?
And where could you find Gushkin-banda of guiltless hands?
For he is the one responsible for making both gods and men
Do you know where Ninagal is, who bears hammer and anvil,

---

[*] Arallu is here a name for the underworld.

Tablet I

Who can bite solid copper as if it were hide, and make tools?
And do you have any idea where the costly stones are found,
Product of the immense sea, which are suitable for crowns?[*]
Do you know where the holy carp, Apsu's Seven Sages are,
Who are unfailing in their great wisdom, as is their lord Ea,
And who are capable of bringing holiness too to my form?"
And the Warlord Erra listened as he stayed, standing there,
And he raised his voice, speaking to King Marduk, saying,
"Then the first Artisans will once again arise from the Apsu,
And the holy *mesu*-tree will once again spread its branches,
As for the holy *elmesu*-stone, **it will shine again in the sun."**
So after Marduk had heard every word that he had spoken,
Thus raising his voice to be heard, said to the Warlord Erra,
"I will go from my house, to bring chaos to Heaven and Earth
The flood-waters will ascend and spread out across the land
And the extensive light of day will become as dark as pitch
The tempest will arise, obscuring every star, Heaven's gems
A vile wind will blow; all people and animals will **be blinded**
Gallu-demons will arise and capture **from among the living**
Them who lack clothing will **rebel against** their oppressors
Thus too will the Anunnaki arise and seek to crush all life!
And before I take up weapons, could any cause them to flee?"
And after Warlord Erra had heard every word spoken to him,
He raised his voice to be heard, speaking to King Marduk,

---

[*] These are likely amber stones

Erra and Ishum

"Then King Marduk, until such time as you go back home,
And Gerra purifies your robes, and you are in your palace,
I will be the emperor and master of both Heaven and Earth,
I will ascend up into Heaven and give commands to the Igigi,
And I will descend into the Apsu and rule over the Anunnaki
I will dispatch the fearsome *gallu*-demons down into Kurnugi
And with my savage weaponry all of them will be subjugated
I will bind fast the pinions of the vile wind as if it were a bird
And at the palace which you will go back to, King Marduk,
There Anu and Ellil will crouch like bulls about your gate!"
Marduk heard every word, and approved of what Erra said.
(So he rose and went forth from his impenetrable dwelling)

TABLET 11

So he rose and went forth from his impenetrable dwelling,[*]
And he went in the direction of the place of the Anunnaki
There he entered **into their assembly** and stood before them
And he shed his brilliance, so that the beams fell **to the tiles;**
As his interest was elsewhere, no more **caring for** the Earth
And there arose **winds,** the light of day turned to darkness:
The wide plains of the countryside as well as **the mountains**
And the flood-waters rose up **from the depths of the Apsu**
Swelling up from the founts and the very bottom **of the sea**
Breaching the entire rim of **the world encircling the ocean**
And the surging torrent ripped clean across the country
Pastures were flooded, valleys inundated, forests uprooted
Then the fury unleashed too struck the fated cities of man
Havoc and unrelenting destruction were the final outcome
Until the waters receded and lands were parched once more
Then all the gods were summoned to the palace of Marduk,
King Marduk was seated upon his high throne, magnified
The crown **of kingship upon his head was shining with light,**
His heart **agleam with the great pride of the world's emperor,**
(And the king of the gods raised his voice to be heard, saying,)
"The Mantle of Brilliance **shines with a breathtaking gleam,**
Thus may Ea of the Apsu **sit up and take notice of this deed**

---

[*] This is Marduk going to initiate a second flood.

89

May Shamash gaze **upon my work,** making the people **pray**
May Sin see it, and through his portent **declare it** to the world
Regarding the work **which everyone regards** Ea to be expert!"
The Warlord Erra was enraged, and spoke to them, saying,
"Was it for the sake of the turbulence upon the water-top
That Marduk established **the law** of mankind, who I made,
To bring the present-offering of the Anunnaki in too soon?
And concocted a plan of evil designed to destroy the world,
To extinguish all the people, **and bring all life to extinction!"**
And King Ea thought about what he said, and in reply spoke,
"Recall that it was King Marduk who stood, giving the decree,
He it was who told the Artisans they were not to arise again
Their statues I constructed among the people for his holiness,
Which no god ever visits or approaches **because of you Erra!"**
(Thus concerning the making of the Artisans' statues by Ea:)
He gave the Artisans a charitable nature, **secur**ed their base,
Gave them wisdom, made their sculptures pleasing to the eye,
Making their robes more rich and brilliant than any hitherto
And the Warlord Erra kept astute guard both day and night
And regardless of what was brought to fashion brilliant robes,
As Marduk the king of all kings ordered, he would simply say,
"Do not go near the statues! **For he who does** I will slaughter!
So too will I prolong his **agonies in the process of killing him**
Thus engage yourselves **in decorating Shamash's statue** now!
To make it brilliant in all its finery such that it has no equal!

90

Then this will be sent down to be among the Earth's people
Such that the honor given to it will rival that of all royalty!
A golden halo on his head, with his robes made to shine!"
Thus the garment makers spun and wove the best of cloth
Coming the next day they clothed King Shamash's statue,
And the temple masons set the foundation of his dwelling
From that day forth the light was established in the world
Then all gods assembled and gave praise to King Marduk[20]

※

The gods' father and astute counselor, Anu called a congress,
Ellil, the gods' father, god of Duranki, made his declaration,
And the gods, every one of them in Heaven, were in agreement,
Even amongst the cattle of Shakkan, all accepted the decision
And of all the gods it was Erra alone who remained in silence
Amongst the heavenly stars, only the Fox Star gave indications
It sparkled and its star-light conveyed special meaning to him
While the constellations of all of the other god shone strongly,
As they were in discord and King Marduk in a tough position,
(And the king of the gods raised his voice to be heard, saying,)
"Erra's star sparkles and sends its light, the omens of Anunitu[*]
His Mantle of Brilliance once triggered causes all beings to die:
Whether it be the gleaming heavenly stars that determine fate,

---

[*] Anunitu is Antu, Anu's wife and Ishtar's mother.

91

Or whether an ant, the mite of creation, it **makes** no **difference**,
Even Shakkan's cattle, whose asterism is the Fox **and Tiller!**[*]
Being full of might, a ferocious lion **can hardly be turned away**
Ellil, as the parent of all populations, has given his final **word."**
Then Innina[†] addressed the gods' congress, giving **wise** counsel
Speaking to Anu and Dagan **relating to the declaration,** saying,
"Listen, all of you! When back in your room cover your mouth
For didn't you smell the **smoke-offering** with King Marduk?[‡]
So neither attempt to give him advice nor try to **persuade him**
Until the task is completed, and the requisite hour has passed
For the utterance of Marduk is alike to the forested mountain
For what he speaks will not be altered **once it has been made!"**
Then Erra **raised his voice to be heard, speaking to Innina,**
"In light of what was spoken before, of adding injury to insult
You know the consequences that would arise if I did the deed
And all life was eradicated from earth, including feeble man
Whatever you might say it will not make a bit of difference."
And Ishtar went forth and they all went to their private rooms,
She attempted to persuade Erra, but he refused **to listen to her**
Then Ishum raised his voice to be heard, speaking to Innina,
"Since he slighted **him Erra is fuming and refuses to keep quiet**
The mountains might be peaceful **but fail** to bring him **peace."**

---

[*] The Babylonian '*Wolf and Plow*' constellation, in proximity to the North Star, was associated with the gain and destruction of wealth. (White 2008: 231)
[†] Innina is another name for Ishtar, Queen of Heaven.
[‡] Apparently covering their mouths so as not to taste the sacrifices being made by man to propitiate them

Tablet II

Ellil's towering son, never marching without Ishum at his lead,
Went to Emeslam[*] and there he made a home for himself
He considered everything pertaining to the matter at hand
Yet within his heart **there was no remedy,** for it answered not
And he questioned himself, asking "How can you just sit idly?
Rather make way that I might set forth upon the highway!
All the required time has gone by, the requisite hour passed,
I avow that I will seek to extinguish the very light of the Sun
So too I avow that I will obscure the Moon's face at midnight
And I will give word to Adad, saying, 'Bottle up your spouts,
Disperse the clouds into the distance, withhold rain and snow.'
Then of both Ea and Marduk will force them to acknowledge:
'He who develops in fruitful years will be interred in scarcity,
He who travels without thirst will find a desert on his return.'
And will say to the gods' king, 'Stay where you are in Esagila!
For no doubt they will obey, and fulfill all that you command
But in failing to hear the people's prayers, they will curse you!'
Then will I devastate the land, deeming it to be forsaken ruins,
And I shall smash cities and turn them back into wild-lands
I will crush the highlands, bringing death to their creatures
I will bring turbulence to the seas, wiping out all their bounty
I will upturn reed beds and burial pits, to burn as Gerra does
I will bring death to all people and all life will be extinguished,

---

[*] 'Meslam abode', meaning the underworld (Erra is sometimes identified with Nergal, king of the underworld)

And I will not withhold a single one **from the mass extinction!**
I will leave not one of Shakkan's cattle or a single wild animal!
And going to every city, I will take captive whoever rules there
And no son will care for his father, and no father for his son
And the mother will gladly seek what is bad for her daughter
And I will permit the bandit to go into a sacrosanct temple,
Wherein the feet of the ungodly sort ought never to tread
And I will let the vagrant take his seat in the house of royalty
And I will cause wild animals **of the plains** to enter shrines
And I will prevent anyone from entering any city he meets
And I will permit the wild beasts of the sierra to enter cities
And I will wreck public squares, anywhere people might be
And I will let beasts of the wild-lands roam in the city center
And I will permit an evil comet to come and decimate the city
And I will allow the Evil-Doer to enter the gods' holy of holies
And I will raze the royal citadel, reducing it to rubble **forever**
And I will make humanity's uproar cease, rob him of all mirth
Alike to **the raging** fires **of war** where peace had once reigned
From every quarter of the world will I allow the evil to come!"
(Staying within his dwelling, he refused to pay heed to anyone)

TABLET III

Staying within his dwelling, he refused to pay heed to anyone,
And all of their persuasive attempts with him **were ignored**
Lions **would be alike to quails compared to the wrath of Erra**
And as his will became more firm, so too did his anger grow
As he felt compelled to **perform the acts which were required,**
"I will make them endure **hardship** and reduce their life-spans
I will strike down the righteous man in the prime of his life
I will set the unrighteous one **upon the throne,** the terminator
I will confuse the people's minds, so the father forgets his son,
And the daughter will tell her mother she ought to go away
I will make them speak in villainy, make them blasphemers,
Forsaking their god, openly declaring their goddess a whore!
I will cause the brigand to arise to make the roads impassible
Even in the center-square, each will ransack the other's things
Both the wolf and lion will bring down the cattle of Shakkan
I will unleash **the *pasittu*-demon** to cut short children's lives
I will bereft the nurse of the bawling infant and tot's chatter
And I will cause Alala* to forsake the grazing pasturelands
Both the shepherd and herder will abandon their sheltering
I will cause the clothes of the man to be shorn from his body
And I will make the youth walk naked in the central-square
I will have the youth enter the underworld without a shroud

---

* Alala is god of the harvest

95

Erra and Ishum

His stocks of sacrificial sheep will die, thus imperiling his life
As for the royal, his flock of lambs will no longer be sufficient
And they will be unable to gain the prophesies of Shamash
The ailing man will accept nothing but savory meat to eat,
He will not accept **anything else offered, rather** he will leave
During the war campaign I will bring royal horses to a halt,
The lifespan of all his entire army of soldiers will I cut short,
And the axles of his chariots will I cause to remain stuck fast[21]

✳

(Ishum raised his voice, speaking to Warlord Erra, saying,)
"You gave arms to the men of peace, a sin to Anu and Dagan,
You caused their blood to flow in the central-square's gutters
You severed their veins and the river washes away the blood
The cry of Ellil has been heard, from his woe-stricken heart
Having left his house, with an incurable curse upon his lips,
He pledged to never again go to the river's waters to drink
He will not touch their blood, and he stays away from Ekur."
Erra spoke to Ishum, he who walks at the vanguard, saying,
"The Sebitti, unrivaled warrior-**gods,** and equally **formidable,**
Are **warlords like Anu,** marching before **the gods' armies,**
Who **like the Flood-weapon bring devastation to the land,**
Who like Gerra **do reduce the countryside to an ashen heap,**
And when appearing at the front door **he is least welcome**

Like **Adad rage without mercy, like Shamash are supreme!**

These are the ones whom Erra **has enlisted to wreak havoc**

There is nothing more fierce than the lion's ferocious maw

And in my fury **I set my sights towards total obliteration!**

Rather make way that I might set forth upon the highway!

I will enlist the matchless warrior-gods, the Sebitti, **to fight**

And they will stride side-by-side with me, my fearsome arms

While you may either march at the vanguard or at the rear."

Ishum heard all his words, and overcome with pity thought,

"My poor people, who Erra sets upon and **is wont to destroy**

Like the warrior Nergal, as in the battle fray, **hacked** Asakku

While his arms, like the ones which **killed** the defeated god,

They are surely yet powerful enough to exterminate them

While his net, like the one used to overcome the evil Anzu,[*]

In just the same way, it has been unfurled to ensnare them."

Ishum raised his voice, speaking to the Warlord Erra, saying,

"Why do you devise vile plans against both man and god?

And although you've settled on this evil scheme against man,

Could you not yet refrain from it, and leave them in peace?"

Erra spoke to Ishum, he who walks at his vanguard, saying,

"You are already aware of what the Igigi have chosen to do,

And likewise that which the Anunnaki have recommended

---

[*] This likely means that Anzu was viewed as being related to the bird-god who makes his first appearance in the historical record on the cave wall of Lascaux known as the 'Birdman'—a myth also recorded in the Mesopotamian myth of 'Etana' (not included here)—which is the constellation of *Orion*. (see *The Eden Enigma*)

You conveyed the order about man, and were well aware of it

Thus how can you talk like someone who is totally unaware?

Dispensing advice as if ignorant of all Marduk did say to me!

Recall that the king of the gods has set forth from his abode,

Put aside his kingly crown, thus will things remain the same?

And the king and royalty **of the land** will forgo the proper rites

Having loosened his belt, thus the restrainer of gods and men

Has become slackened and is no more fit to be girded anew

Gerra, in a passion, made his robe glow as the day in brilliance

Holding aloft a mace in his right hand, his superlative weapon

Know that the gaze of King Marduk is frightening to behold

And even so do you speak to me **of holding back my strength?**

O astute Ishum, who guides the gods, giving unrivalled advice,

How can you sit there and **speak of withholding from action?**

Was the command of Marduk not what you wanted to hear?"

Ishum raised his voice, speaking to the Warlord Erra, saying,

"O Warlord Erra, **where do you see the benefit of doing this?**

To crush the people down and **bring devastation to all lands**

Even the prairie where the cattle of Shakkan **are given to graze,**

The reed bed and forest which **serve as nesting place for foul**

Then considering what you're saying Warlord Erra, **you know**

Only one gets supreme command, but you **went your own way**

From among seven you killed every last one, not sparing one

Cattle **were stricken where they stood, wild beasts massacred**

O Erra, when you strike your weapons against one another,

Tablet III

Then do the mountain-sides tremble and the oceans rise up
All turn their gaze to the peak when your sword **blade** gleams
While the citadel **set upon the flatland topples to the ground**

※

Ishum raised his voice, speaking to the Warlord Erra, saying,
"O Warlord Erra, you who grasp firmly the reigns of Heaven,
Hold dominion over the land, and command all of the Earth,
You brought violence to the ocean, you encircled mountains
You are the lord over the people and the master of all beasts
Esharra awaits your orders; E-engurra is yours to command,
You are the guardian of Shuanna, the monarch of Esagila[*]
You are the one who declares the rites and all gods honor you
You are praised by the Igigi and respected by the Anunnaki,
And affirmed by Ellil. Can chaos be without your intervention,
Or any conflict break out when you yourself are not present?
While the entire battle arsenal is completely at your disposal
Still you think to yourself, 'They hold only contempt for me!'
(Warlord Erra, have you no fear for King Marduk's name?)

---

[*] These are all temples or temple locations

99

TABLET IV

Warlord Erra, have you no fear for King Marduk's name?
You have undone the bind bonding the city of Dimkurkurra
The city of the gods' king, which is the binding of the world!*
You've altered your godly nature into something humanlike!
You've taken up your arms and entered Babylon's very center,
Proclaiming, like a boaster, that you would conquer that city
While the sons of Babylon, who have no one fit to lead them,
Have rather rallied to you like they were reeds in a reed bed
The one without knowledge of weapons unsheathes his blade
The one without knowledge of archery strings sinew to bow
The one without knowledge of war goes onto the battlefield
The one without feathers is taking to the air as though a bird
The man with no muscles is overwhelming the strong man
The one who is laden down in fatness is surpassing the swift
And no small insults are being hurled at the temple warden
Their hands did barricade Babylon's gate, its very lifeblood,
Like highwaymen they tossed torches into Babylon's temples
Heading their ranks, you lead the battle charge into the fray,
Sending arrows upon Imgur-Ellil until he cries, "Woe is me!"†
As for Muhra, the city's gatekeeper, you laid the foundation
Of his home in the blood of both their youths and maidens‡

---

* Dimkurkurra meaning here Babylon, the city of Marduk
† Imgur-Ellil is Babylon's defensive wall
‡ Muhra is the bi-faced guardian of the underworld's gates.

Tablet IV

For the citizens of Babylon you are the draw and they the fowl;
Caught in your net, you seized and killed them, Warlord Erra!
You abandoned the city limits and went to god-knows-where
You took on the visage of the lion and entered the royal home
The army recognized you and took up their weapons for war
The chief administrator, once Babylon's benefactor, went mad
And issued orders to his men to pillage like foreign raiders
You encouraged the general to commit vile offences, saying,
'I designate you as the one whom I will dispatch into the city!
And you will show no consideration for either man or god,
Rather wipe out both old and young without discrimination
No infant will be left alive, even those at their mother's breast,
And then you shall plunder all the collected riches of Babylon.'
Thus as the king's men, ranked into squads, stormed the city,
The bow-string was plucked and the sword blade was poked
You gave arms to the men of peace, a sin to Anu and Dagan
You caused their blood to flow in the central-square's gutters
You severed their veins and the river washes away the blood
The cry of Marduk was heard, from his woe-stricken heart
Having left his house, with an incurable curse upon his lips,
He pledged to never again go to the river's waters to drink
He will not touch their blood, and stays away from Esagila

And then King Marduk raised his voice to be heard, saying,
'O poor Babylon, founding you as majestic as the date-palm,

Erra and Ishum

Yet from such heights the wind has reduced you to nothing

O poor Babylon, making you full like the seeds of a pinecone,

Yet even from such great plentitude there came no harvest

O poor Babylon, like a fruitful orchard when I planted you,

Yet from this never came a single piece of fruit I might savor

O poor Babylon, which I myself set around the neck of Anu,

And hung about his neck like the *elmesu*-stone cylinder seal

O poor Babylon, taken into my hands like the Tablet of Fate,

And refuse to permit it to be put into the hands of another.'

And then King Marduk raised his voice to be heard, saying,

'**Gone are those things** which **have stood** for all recorded time

So from now on he who would go by boat must travel on foot

From now on the rope put into the pit is no man's salvation

From now on the ocean-going fishing boat will go 100 leagues

Out in the midst of the vastness of the ocean with just a pole

Even the city that has stood since the advent of time, Sippar,

That the World's Ruler, so fond of it, saved from the Flood,

You toppled its walls even without the approval of Shamash

And beyond this you smashed and scattered its fortifications

And even within the city of Uruk, where Anu and Ishtar live,

That urban bed of mistresses, courtesans, and street whores

Ishtar made it bereft of husbands, who fell under their spell

While Sutean men and women shout their abusive language[*]

---

[*] The Suteans were nomadic raiders who attacked Babylonian cities in the 11th century BC and likely continued to be viewed as their traditional enemies. (Dalley 2000: 282)

Tablet IV

The festive boys and pageant group bring Eanna to fever pitch

Who changed themselves, making their maleness femaleness,

And by so doing to persuade Ishtar's people to venerate her[*]

And as for the blade-holders, the carriers of sharp daggers,

Who go about with the scalping knife and the sharp flint,

Who often perform the shameful act that brings Ishtar joy,

You appointed an unworthy administrator who abuses them

Rather he hunted them down and desecrated their rituals

Thus Ishtar was furious and became spiteful against Uruk

So he brought in a foreign army and ruined the countryside

Just as mature wheat-stalks are flattened by the flood-surge

While the lamenting rituals of Parsay's people never stopped

All for the sake of E-ugal, which had been ruthlessly violated,[†]

As the foreign army you'd called in simply refused to cease.'

And then Angal himself raised his voice to be heard, saying,

'You have made the city of Der to stand empty as a wasteland,[‡]

You have shattered those who live there as if they were reeds!

You have brought their tumult to an end, like oil stills ripples

Even I was not spared, as you handed me over to the Suteans

Thus such will I do, in remembrance of my dear city of Der:

I will no longer deal out justice, will no longer regulate lands

I will dispense with all commands, not listen to a single word

---

[*] Speaking of the worship of Ishtar, and Eanna is her temple in Uruk
[†] Parsay is a city near Baghdad and E-ugal is the name of Ellil's temple there
[‡] Angal is the patron god of Der, also known as Ishtaran.

Erra and Ishum

As people have forsaken justice, and taken to committing sins,

They have recanted all virtuous conduct and plot only vile acts

Thus I caused the seven winds to strike against this single land

And any not losing his life in battle will meet death by disease

And any not dead of disease, the foreigners will take as a slave

And any who have not met death from the hands of a bandit

He will find himself brought down by the emperor's sword

And any spared by the emperor's sword, Adad will wipe out

And any whom Adad has not obliterated, Shamash will scorch

Any who travel the countryside will be plagued by the wind

Any who comes back to his home will the Deadly Stalker strike

And any who makes his way into the hills, he will die of thirst

And any who makes his way into the valleys, he will drown

For you hold influence in both the highest and lowest places

The city administrator will be heard to say to she that bore him,

"If only I had stuck in your womb the day you gave birth to me,

If only my life had been cut off and we'd both died at that time

For you bore me in a city which must witness its walls topple,

To see its people reduced to cattle and their god as a predator

His net is so finely woven, that even worthy men were unable

To raise their swords, and were themselves slain by the sword."

And the father of a son will be heard to say, "This is my son,

The son I reared, and thus does he perform acts of kindness."

But the son I will slay and his father be the one who inters him

Then following this I will strike the father down with death,

And there will be no one to perform the internment for him
While he who has built himself a house, and says, "My house,
Now that I have finished it, will rest content within its walls
And on the day I am taken by Fate I will settle there eternally."[*]
I will strike him down with death and obliterate his house,
And then, after its desolation, will make it a gift to another!'

O Warlord Erra, you have stricken with death the righteous,
And likewise you have stricken with death the unrighteous
You have stricken with death both the one who offended you,
And have stricken with death the one who did not offend you
You killed the *en*-priest who made present-offerings on time
You have stricken with death the noble who advised the king
You have stricken the elderly man with death upon his porch
You have brought death to the maiden within her bedroom
Yet even after all of this you have not taken a single reprieve
Still you think to yourself, 'They hold only contempt for me!'
Then, Warlord Erra, do you speak in this manner to yourself,
'I will strike down the man of strength and panic the weakling
I will assassinate the general and bring about his army's end
I will cause the shrine which sits atop the temple to be fouled,
As well as the battlements, and bring an end to all city life
I will rip free the anchor poles so the boats will go down-river
I will split the rudder that it will not be able to come to shore

---

[*] That is, to be interred beneath his house, as was commonly done.

Erra and Ishum

I will tear out the mast pole and bring down all of its rigging

I will dry the woman's breasts, such that the babe must perish

I will hold back founts, so ditches can't bring refreshing water

I will bring a tremor to Erkalla such that the very sky quavers

I will make Jupiter no longer shine, and discard Heaven's stars

The trees' roots will be severed that new shoots cannot thrive

I will smash the wall's foundation such that its top will falter

I will go to the gods' king, that reason will not rule the day!'"

And the Warlord Erra heard every word that he spoke to him

And Ishum's speech was as pleasing to him as purified oil

And the Warlord Erra raised his voice to be heard, saying,

"Thus the people of the sea will not spare people of the sea,

Nor will Subartian spare Subartian, nor Assyrian Assyrian,

Nor will Elamite spare Elamite, nor will Kassite spare Kassite,

Nor will Sutean spare Sutean, nor will Gutian spare Gutian,

Nor Lullubean Lullubean, nor country country, nor city city,

Nor will the tribe spare the tribe, nor will the man the man,

Nor will brother spare brother, but rather will kill each other

Yet following all of this will arise a man from out of Akkad,

And he will destroy all of them, and then guide the survivors."[*]

Warlord Erra spoke to Ishum, he who walks at his vanguard,

"Set forth, Ishum! And pay heed to the words which you spoke!"

Thus Ishum set off in the direction of the mountain of Hehe,

---

[*] This marks the key revelation of the myth, in which a future savior is portended by Erra; although it is not clear who this figure might have been, it may be Nabonassar or Merodach-Baladan. (Dalley 2000: 283)

Tablet IV

The Sebitti, matchless warrior-gods, raising dust in his wake

The warrior came to mount Hehe, lifted his hand and crushed it,

Then he considered the mountain to be a plain from henceforth

And then within the cypress-wood forest, he hacked the trunks,

Like **barley stalks left shorn in the field after the harvest cutting**

He obliterated all of the cities, turning them into a wasteland

He crushed the highlands, bringing death to their creatures

He brought turbulence to the seas, wiping out all their bounty

He upturned reed beds and burial pits, to burn as Gerra does

He made it so that the cattle were stricken, and reverted to clay.

(When Erra refrained and once again returned to his house)

TABLET V

When Erra refrained and once again returned to his house
Then every one of the gods was given to stare upon his face
Both the Igigi and Anunnaki, every one of them, stood in awe
Then Erra raised his voice to be heard, speaking to all gods,
"Everyone remain silent, and listen to the words that I speak!
Even if I had meant every unprovoked act I did to be baleful,
When I am angered I manifest my wrath against the people
As the flock's keeper, I draw the head sheep out of the pen,
As one who didn't plant an orchard, I readily cut one down
Just as the one who strikes forth to pillage the countryside,
I do not discern righteous from unrighteous; both are slain
One does not steal a carcass from the jaws of a hunting lion
When one is insane, another cannot make him see reason!
And what if Ishum, who walks at my vanguard, were absent?
Then where would your donor be, and where your *en*-priest?
Likewise, where would you go to receive your food-offerings?
And you wouldn't even be able to smell the smoke-offering!"
Ishum raised his voice, speaking to the Warlord Erra, saying,
"O Warlord, sit back and hear the words I am about to speak!
Consider the option to refrain, and we will act as your servants
We all see that none might challenge you in your hour of fury!"
When Erra heard the words he spoke, his face was glowing
The traits of his face took on the aspect of a new day's dawn

Tablet V

And he went into Emeslam and there retired within his home

Then Ishum made the pronouncement, declared the judgment,

Giving the decision regarding the remnant of Akkad's people,

"Let the lessened people across the land regain their numbers

Let the men of every walk of life again go about their business

Let Akkad's weak man be able to overcome the strong Sutean;

Let one man be able to repel seven like they were a flock of fowl:

You will obliterate their cities, leave their orchards in desolation

Then you will make their bounteous wealth flow into Shuanna

Place the land's once wrathful gods back where they belong

You will allow Shakkan and Nissaba to descend to the Earth

Let the highlands generate riches, bring on the ocean's bounty

Allow the meadows you had ravaged to be fruitful once again,

That the rulers of every city transport its treasures to Shuanna!

May the temples, fallen into disrepair, rise as the noonday sun

May the Tigris and Euphrates convey their waters in plentitude

May all cities' rulers give to the patron of Esagila and Babylon!"

Let praises ring out for the almighty Nergal and warrior Ishum

For countless ages to come; how Erra had once become enraged

And sought to destroy the land and obliterate all of its people

But Ishum, his advisor, calmed him so he did not destroy all!

Epilogue

(The Warlord Erra was greatly pleased with this song and said:)[*]

"May riches flow into the temple of any god who extols this song!

While the one who dismisses it will not savor the smoke-offering!

The king who glorifies my name will rule over the entire world,

Royalty who recount the honor accorded my valor be supreme

The minstrel found singing it will never meet death by plague,

Its lyrics will be well-known amongst the kings and all royalty

The life of the scribe who copies it will be saved in enemy lands,

And will find that his countrymen bestow great honors on him

Even in the artisans' shrine, where they ever invoke my name,

They will gain wisdom; in whatever dwelling the tablet resides

Even when Erra proves irate and the Sebitti rage like a tempest,

Death's scythe will not touch; he has been granted peace forever

May this song last evermore, may it survive for all time to come!

That every land will hear it and give honor to my valiant deeds,

And that all the civilized world will know and glorify my name!"

---

[*] The following speech is included upon the tablets after disclosing the traditional source of the myth and Erra's approval of its composition.

Bibliography

Betz, Hans Dieter, ed. <u>The Greek Magical Papyri in Translation: Including the Demotic Spells</u>. Vol 1. 1986. Chicago: University of Chicago, 1992.

Coogan, Michael David. <u>Stories from Ancient Canaan</u>. Louisville: Westminster, 1978.

Dalley, Stephanie, trans. <u>Myths from Mesopotamia</u>. 1989. New York: Oxford, 2000.

Frazer, James George. <u>The Golden Bough: A New Abridgement</u>. 1994. New York: Oxford, 1998.

Kramer, Samuel and. Diane Wolkstein. <u>Inanna: Queen of Heaven and Earth</u>. New York: Harper & Row, 1983.

Olcott, William Tyler. <u>Star Lore: Myths, Legends, and Facts</u>. 1911. New York: Dover, 2004.

Stephany, Timothy J. <u>Enuma Elish: The Babylonian Creation Epic</u>. printed by Createspace, 2014.

Stephany, Timothy J. <u>Blood & Incest: The Unholy Beginning of the Universe</u>. printed by Createspace, 2014.

Stephany, Timothy J. <u>Roar of the Tempests: A Dialogue</u>. printed by Createspace, 2014.

Stephany, Timothy J. <u>The Eden Enigma: A Dialogue</u>. printed by Createspace, 2014.

Stephany, Timothy J. <u>The Gilgamesh Cycle</u>. printed by Createspace, 2014.

White, Gavin. <u>Babylonian Star-Lore</u>. London: Solaria, 2008.

Endnotes

[1] Kramer (1983), p. 101.

[2] Kramer (1983), p. 103.

[3] Kramer (1983), p. xvi.

[4] 'Enuma Elish', Tablet VI

[5] Dalley (2000), p. 160.

[6] Kramer (1983), p. 142.

[7] Roar of the Tempests, p. 180.

[8] Olcott (2004), p. 278.

[9] see Hartner, Willy, "The Earliest History of the Constellations in the Near East and the Motif of the Lion-Bull Conflict." *Journal of Near Eastern Studies*, 12, pp. 1-16, 1965.

[10] Kramer (1983), p. 150; see Frazer (1998), pp. 659-660.

[11] Dalley (2000), p. 154.

[12] Kramer (1983), pp. 124-125.

[13] Kramer (1983), p. 154.

[14] Blood and Incest, p. 162.

[15] Frazer (1998), pp. 658-665.

[16] Following Kramer (1983) 'Dumuzi's Dream' also contains supplementary material from the fragmentary myth 'Dumuzi and Geshtinanna'.

[17] This section constitutes songs of lamentation provided by Kramer (1983), prior to the conclusion of 'From the Great Above' commencing, when Geshtinanna next appears, with a gap of about 20 lines.

[18] Here is a lacuna of about 50 lines, absent or fragmentary.

[19] There are about 25 lines missing at the end. In the earlier lacuna there may have been two attempted offers made to Nimrod by Ellil in return for his deed, with Nimrod turning them both down. The remaining fragmentary ending is superficially incomplete and lacks a conclusion, which under this scenario would be Nimrod's acceptance of Ellil's third offer of absolute supremacy.

[20] There follows a significant gap of about 35 lines, perhaps detailing the recollection of how each of the god's statues within the temples were prepared under the watchful eye of Marduk. When it commences again Ellil has formulated and made a proposal before the gods, which Erra appears to be opposed to.

[21] About 45 lines following are missing

Printed in Great Britain
by Amazon